Franz Kafka
and
Literary Modernism

Franz Kafka
and
Literary Modernism

Mallikarjun Patil

GNOSIS

Nurturing the Aspirations

Introduction

Franz Kafka was a modernist. He was a neo-romanticist, expressionist and surrealist. The existentialist thinkers claimed that he was an atheist existentialist. No doubt, he was influenced by both Soren Kierkegaard and Martin Heidegger.

The 1950s practioners of the Theatre of the Absurd found a lot of similarity between Kafka and themselves. Absurd novelist Albert Camus modelled his work *The Outsider* on Kafka's novel *The Trial.* Martin Esslin found Kafka's writings as an embodiment of modern man's anxiety, dread and purposelessness.

Franz Kafka is considered as a neo-romanticist. This is really interesting. Like the romantic writers he yearned for subjectivity and the exotic. He played with man's rich imagination. His novella *The Metamorphosis* is an example of this.

Kafka is an expressionist writer. Expressionism was a German movement in literature and other arts in Kafka's own time. So Kafka, as an expressionist, depicted the visionary, emotional and distorted.

As a surrealist, Kafka wrote of the world. He was disgusted with the Christian attitude towards Jews, the German-Czech conflicts, man's own fear and anguish, and God's indifference to man. Most of his novels and stories show an artistic deviation – a journey into the imaginary world.

In this background Kafka emerges as a powerful modern writer. He wrote novels like *America, The Trial, The Castle,* and *The Metamorphosis.* He has written numerous short stories like "In the Penal Colony." His three novels read like 'a trilogy of loneliness' as his friend and editor, Max Brod, says. His fiction reflects the experience of human isolation and the pathos of exclusion. His works whether novels, stories, letters, diaries or aphorisms provide us an excellent worldview of Germany in the first quarter of the twentieth century. His style is characterized by an extensive use of religious symbolism, compactness, intensity, grotesque/nightmarish scenes—rather surrealistic. He reminds us Poe, Chaplin, Disney and Dickens.

The present book on Kafka is a critical monograph for Indian readers. The book has as many as seven chapters. The first chapter is an introduction to Kafka. Since Kafka was a modernist writer, the second chapter discusses modernism at Kafka's time. Chapter 3 is a critical analysis of Kafka novels; and Chapter 4 of his short stories. Kafka was a fine letter writer, and even a diarist, as can be seen in the next chapter. Kafka was obsessed with many subjects that harassed the modern man; he worried about the Christians' anti-semetic attitude, capitalism and this is discussed in Chapter 6. As a great writer Kafka is compared with great people like Kierkegaard, Freud, Dickens, etc., in the next chapter.

Contents

1
Franz Kafka's Life

Franz Kafka is one of the greatest writers.

Kafka was born as a Jew and German in Prague on 3 July 1883. Now Prague is the capital city of Czechoslovakia. This is a puzzling phenomenon for us as it was for Kafka then. He lived in an indifferent world with an indifferent father, German hostility, because his mother tongue was German. He wanted to become a writer, while writing yielded him no livelihood, and he wanted a happy life, yet he suffered immensely from ill-health. He wanted love that eluded him at last. His life was really intriguing.

The peculiar flavour of his books, the now universalized 'Kafkaesque,' derives from this sense of being unhoused, unable to find accommodation in a mysteriously antagonistic world. From guilt, but like Joseph K in *The Trial,* Kafka felt himself to be an accused without a formal accusation, a criminal without a crime. From exclusion, like the land surveyor who cannot breach the baffling protocols of *The Castle* in order to establish himself in its orbit. From hope for a new life and a personal remaking, like the hero of *The Man Who Disappeared (America)*.

Europe, at the turn of the twentieth century, was an unstable and turbulent place. Kafka was producing his writing during and in the aftermath of World War I, and, with stories like "In the Penal Colony," would weave that influence into his words. "As a writer, Kafka's affinities first lay with the decadent *fin-de-siècle,* then veered towards the violence associated with Expressionism, and finally reached a mode closer to the unadorned starkness typified by German *New Sobriety*."

As J. Adler writes, "Europe was a changing place. The advance of technology, intellectual ideas and fashion made it an exciting place to be. Change was very much the flavor of the day. Prague was, according to the writer and artist Andre Breton, regarded as the 'secret capital of Europe,' and '... a place where, politically, a new century was forged, and all the arts flourished.' "

In amongst the political turmoil of the time, the continuing hostilities concerning the Jews and the advance of war, Prague maintained the strong intellectual heart. The Prague Circle, the group that Kafka was associated with, drank and discussed long into the evening. The group included writers such as Frank Werfel, Ergon Kisch, Hugo Bergmann, Otto Pick, Ernst Pollak and Max Brod.

Still Kafka lived a satisfactory life. He wrote a good deal of fiction. Once he passed away, his friend Max Brod edited and published his works. In the mid twentieth century, the existentialists and absurdists claimed him as their pioneer. Now Kafka is a modernist.

The Kafkas were Jews. His grandfather Jacob (1814-89) was a butcher from Osek, Bohemia. The Kafkas spoke Yiddish, Czech and German. Jakob's wife Franziska bore six children in poverty. The fourth child Hermann settled down in Prague. He adopted Kafka (Kavka in Czech) as a surname (which symbolized Jews' suffering). Kafka's mother Julie came from a textile and brewery trade in Podiebrad-upon-Elbe.

Julie's father, a Talmud scholar, also moved to Prague. Her other relatives were Rudolf, Alfred and Joseph Lowy. These Lowy uncles influenced Kafka's novel *The Man Who Disappeared*. Some of these uncles—Alfred (director of the Spanish railways), Siegfried (a doctor in Moravia) and Rudolf (a book-keeper)—got converted to Christianity. Kafka's father was rough and his mother, very sensible, and Franz had a close bond with her. As Max Brod writes: "Franz's mother loves him very much, but she has not the faintest idea who her son is and what his needs are."

Kafka was born and brought up in this city. As his friend Johannes Urzidill thinks, "Kafka was Prague and Prague was Kafka." Kafka said to his teacher Friedrick Thieberger that his father's home "Minute House" had contained his whole life.

Herman had just quit his army job, and started a fancy goods shop. Julie described Franz as a delicate but healthy child. Then three sisters—Gabriele (Elli), Valerie (Vallie) and Ottilie (Otla)—were born. Otla was his favourite. The parents were busy at the shop and the maids looked after the children with indifference.

Franz began his schooling at age six in 1889 at the Deutsche Knabenschule. His studies were in German as it was the state language. Yet national, linguistic and ethnic conflicts increased between the Germans and the Czechs. Then Prague was ruled from Vienna. The Jews owned industries and the Czechs were workers. In 1900 the social tensions increased after World War I. The Austro-Hungarian Empire collapsed, followed by the formation of the new nation Czechoslovakia headed by Thomas Masaryk. In 1900 the Jews were just 7 per cent in Prague and they lived in the mainstream. They constituted a kind of cultural apartheid.

Controversy broke out in Prague in 2000 when the city council proposed to rename the tiny square in front of Kafka's birthplace Franze Kafky Namesti (Franz Kafka Square). There were objections from the local mayor, and Marta Zelezna of the Franz Kafka Society told the BBC that the city has "an ambivalent relationship" with its most famous writer. "He's not viewed as 'our' writer because he was Jewish and because he wrote in German." Banned in the communist era as decadent, Kafka's work is only now being brought out in a complete Czech translation. The square was renamed, but the ambivalence lingers.

Certainly Kafka was an exception, speaking Czech, as will be seen later, and taking an interest in the Czech language and culture. What should really concern us here is the extent to which this experience of growing up in a rather rarefied, separate world added still further to his natural disposition to feel alienated from his surroundings. In particular, language was a central issue. Kafka, though in no sense an ideological writer, always had a keen political awareness, sympathy for the underdog and a mistrust of the powerful.

The ten-year-old Franz joined the German Gymnasium. He studied Greek, Latin and Maths. His favourite teacher was Adolf Gottward. Kafka made only a few friends like Hugo Bergmann, the Zionist philosopher; Rudolf Illowy, the socialist thinker; Ewald Pribram, whose father was helpfully president of the insurance firm where Kafka would later work; and Oskar Pollak, the art historian. Bergmann recalls that Kafka was a rebel. Kafka read *Der Kunstwart,* a socialist magazine which influenced Nietzsche. Kafka was a good arguer.

Kafka's classmate Hugo Hecht says Kafka was 'a pure boy,' well-dressed, and also 'distant' from others. Still Kafka wrote: "'When I think about it, I must say that my education has done me great harm in some respects. This reproach applies to a multitude of people, that is to say, my parents, several relatives, individual visitors to our house, various writers, a certain particular cook who took me to school for a year, a crowd of teachers. . . a school inspector, slowly walking passersby; in short this reproach twists through society like a dagger."

Hermann's rough, vigorous handling of the ultrasensitive boy, in order to fashion him in his own likeness as a tough survivor in the battle of life, was not flexible enough even if the harried businessman could have found the time to devote to the task to accommodate the special demands made by his son.

Kafka claimed that what he needed was "a little encouragement, a little friendliness." Hermann urged his son to eat heartily, drink beer with his meals and repeat drinking songs – "but nothing of this had anything to do with Kafka's future." He grumbled: "What I got from you ... was a hesitant, stammering mode of speech, and even that was too much for you, and finally I kept silence, at first perhaps from defiance, and then because I couldn't either think or speak in your presence. And because you were the person who really brought me up," this has had its repercussions throughout his life.

Kafka says still his mother was not to guard the children from the father.

In November 1901 Kafka began his studies at the German Ferdinand Karl University in Prague. This intensely literary 18 year-old who had barely scraped through the mathematical part of the Gymnasium syllabus, and only with Bergmann's help joined Hugo in lectures in chemistry. But soon both left chemistry: Bergamann switched over to maths, and Kafka to law. Kafka attended literature classes also. Prague University founded in 1348, had both factions – German and Czech. It was here, in Kafka's second year, that the aspiring writer Max Brod, who was to play such a defining role in Kafka's life and in the forging of his posthumous literary reputation, first met Kafka. Brod—seen as a dazzlingly clever law student, musician, poet and future novelist—provoked an argument when he described Nietzsche as a fraud.

Kafka was jolly at the university. He had an attractive personality. Fred Berence, a contemporary Swish writer, says, Kafka was tall, well built, very dark haired, extremely dark eyes which smiled. He had a child's face, and was less immature sexually as per his age until 20. Intellectually too he was uncertain and confused as a teenager. During the summer the Kafkas had received a visit from Uncle Alfred Lowy, who was by now Director-General of the Spanish railways, and whose breath of abroad blew into the constrained interior of the Kafka's first-floor apartment at No. 3 Celetna, in the house known as 'At the Three Kings.' This was where Kafka lived with his family from 1896 to 1907, by which time he was 24. At one stage, he wanted to attend studies at the University of Munich, which his father did not allow.

Of much more significance in these first undergraduate years was the fact that Kafka was beginning to exhibit, in letters to friends, hints of the writer to come. He had begun writing in his early teens. He studied law in the second year seriously. His reading was proceeding apace. He had spent the summer of 1903 reading the work of the German philosopher Gustav Fechner (1801-87) and the medieval German mystic Meister Eckhart. As the third year commenced he concentrated more exclusively on law, having put behind him the courses on German literature and language, the history of art, music, psychology and classical philology.

It would be wrong, however, to conclude that Kafka led a wholly monastic existence. In July 1903 his first sexual encounter—typically for a young man of his class—was with a working-class Czech girl. The sexual urge forced him for sex either with prostitutes or other women. He says, "This urge had in it something of the eternal Jew, being senselessly drawn, wandering senselessly through a senselessly obscene world."

Kafka as told to his friend Oskar Pollak in 1903, read voraciously. He said, "I think we ought to read only the kind of books that wound and stab us. If the book we are reading doesn't wake us up with a blow on the head, what are we reading it for? . . .we need the books that affect us like a disaster, that grieve us deeply, like the death of someone we loved more than ourselves, like being banished into forests far from everyone, like a suicide. A book must be the axe for the frozen sea inside us." He read Hebbel (1813-63), Goethe, Mann, Flaubert and others. He began the first of the surviving piece "Description of a Struggle" in 1904.

Kafka's language was quite different from that of his fellow Prague Germans. It has already been noted how isolated politically and sociologically the Prague Germans were from their Czech neighbours. Kafka was exceptional in taking a genuine interest in Czech culture and language; he even subscribed to a Czech philological journal. His concise, neutral, sparse, logically constructed language was a repudiation of the mannered excess of such writers as Gustav Meyrink and Rilke. Nevertheless, it is clear that Kafka, notwithstanding his respect for Czech language and culture, elected to see himself as a German writer and his models were the classical German writers Goethe, Kleist and Stifter.

Kafka was social enough to attend various club meetings and lectures. He had an interest in the Young People's Club, a centre for anarchist youth founded in 1900, staged political lectures in Prague between 1903 and 1910 which attracted the attention of the police. Another claim on Kafka's social self was the elite cafe society of Prague, where philosophy, politics, literature and just about everything else were discussed. At the Cafe Louvre followers of the philosopher Franz Brentano gathered, and several of his disciples, Anton Marty, Oskar Kraus and Alfred Kastil, were teachers at the university. Brentano's ideas were discussed at the famous Prague salon of Berta Fanta. Fanta was the wife of a leading Prague pharmacist whose daughter married Kafka's school friend Hugo Bergmann in 1908. Her imposing house 'At the Unicorn' can still be seen today dominating the Old Town Square. It became a meeting place of the German elite who discussed Brentano and other philosophers such as Fichte, Kant and Hegel. They ventured into more fashionable esoteric areas such as spiritualism, Indian wisdom, Madame Blavatsky and Rudolf Steiner's theosophy. Writers such as Meyrink, Franz Werfel, Willy Haas, Max Brod and Kafka attended, as did the scientist Albert Einstein and the physicist Gerhard Kowaleski. The young conductor Otto Klemperer and the poet Rainer Maria Rilke graced the salon.

In Kafka's letters at this time there are fleeting references to 'prostitutes', an 'Indian dancing girl', and "the twenty-three year-old girl... who provided me with a miracle of a Sunday."

After this, Kafka plunged into his final academic year of legal studies through the autumn and winter of 1904 to 1905. In the summer of 1905 he rewarded himself with a trip to a small town Zuckmantel in Moravian Silesia. Kafka enjoyed the beauty of nature, and also the company of women.

In 1905 Kafka was awarded his doctor of law degree by Professor Alfred Weber (brother of the renowned sociologist). Once his education was over, he was to find out a job. After August in Zuckmantel, Kafka returned to Prague to do one year's mandatory work experience as a lawyer in the courts. Concluding wisely that "my future is not rosy," Kafka set off for Triesch, where he spent August 1907. There he aspired for the companionship of one girl Hedwing Therese Weiler, the first lover to be undentified. The correspondence with Hedwig would continue for two years.

Summer dalliance was all very well, but with the arrival of autumn came the need to find a permanent job. "I need no occupation, the more so since I am not capable of it," he joked rather desperately to Brod, but a job was certainly necessary. He toyed with the idea of attending the Export Academy at Vienna and learning Spanish, in addition to his French and English. Perhaps Uncle Alfred would find an opening for them both in Spain "or else we would go to South America or the Azores, to Madeira." On 1 October 1907 the 24 year-old Kafka started work at the office of the Italian insurance company Assicurazioni Generali. He thus became another of those writer-clerks who have figured so largely in the history of literary modernism—one thinks of Borges, Eliot and Stevens—and whose work was done in the interstices of an office career.

Kafka was hoping eventually for one of the attractive public sector jobs where a shift began early and ended by two or three in the afternoon, leaving time, after a period of recuperation, to write in the evening. The Assicurazioni offices, in Wenceslas Square, were a relatively short walk from the new family home at No. 36 Niklasstrasse, where the Kafkas had moved in June. In this flat, he wrote the great stories "The Judgment" and "The Metamorphosis." The Assicurazioni, according to Franz Baumer, "presented a classical image of dusty Austro-Hungarian bureaucracy."

A medical examination for the job revealed that Kafka was six feet tall and weighed just over sixty kilos. The doctors found him 'healthy' but 'fragile.' His "tiny salary of 80 crowns and an infinite eight to nine hours of work" meant that he was compelled to "devour the hours outside the office like a wild beast." The work was certainly dreary.

In 1909 he finished one piece "The Wedding Preparations in the Country." Meanwhile, something had to be done to create more time to write. Kafka began to see if he could pull a few strings to secure a job at the post office, where the working hours would be shorter, but that came to nothing, and the new year 1908 brought only further office gloom. And the beginning of 1908 brought a fine compensation, his first publication. The bimonthly magazine *Hyperion*, edited by Franz Blei, published in its January issue eight of the very short prose pieces that would later form part of Kafka's first book, *Betrachtung (Meditation* or *Reflection),* published in 1913.

Brod's friendship was a source of great strength for Kafka. He joked with him about a plan to start their nightlife at five o'clock in the morning.

On 15 July Kafka quit the Assicurazioni and on the 30th joined the Arbeiter-Unfall-Versicherungs-Anstalt fur das Konigreich Bohmen in Prag (the Workers' Accident Insurance Institute for the Kingdom of Bohemia in Prague, henceforth 'the Institute'). In his two letters of application, one written in German and the other in Czech, Kafka was keen to stress that he was fluent in spoken and written Czech, as well as competent in French and English. Ten years later, when the Czechoslovakian Republic was founded, Kafka's fluency in Czech would ensure that he kept his job in spite of being a German. This was a semi-public firm. Kafka's job concerned the prevention of industrial accidents and appeals by employers against classification of trades under various categories of risk. He drafted responses to the frequently heated challenges by employers against their high-risk classifications, wrote policy and publicity documents, and represented the Institute in court.

Although Kafka always claimed that he was not very good at his job, this was not the opinion of his employers, who promoted him several times. Kafka was popular in the office, though colleagues noted his boyish demeanour, as if he were not quite fully grown-up. They nicknamed him 'our office baby' and Brod confirmed that there was a certain naivety in his make-up.

On the other hand, in the rough and tumble of the workplace, Kafka learned precisely those lessons of ordinary life that he needed to learn. Inevitably, his immersion in red tape and officialdom has been seen as the inspiration for the bureaucratic nightmares of *The Trial*. His work involved a certain amount of travel, and within a couple of months he was already sending postcards back to Brod from such places as Tetschen on the Elbe.

Kafka was known to be a vegetarian and avoided sausages and pies, bringing instead a buttered roll, which he ate with yoghurt or milk. From 4 to 14 September 1909 Kafka, Brod and Brod's brother, Otto, took a holiday together at the Italian resort of Riva on Lake Garda. On the 11th, they saw an aeroplane show at Brescia. Kafka's account, "The Aeroplanes at Brescia," published in *Bohemia* on 29 September, was the result of a proposal that Brod and he should write rival accounts of the same. Though not the first account of an air show it captures a moment of excitement at a new phenomenon of twentieth-century life.

Towards the end of 1909 Kafka began to keep a diary or notebook whose first entries date from the summer of that year. In 1910, he began feeling bad about his health. His biographer Nicholas Murray observes, "For the rest of his short life Kafka would struggle with the inescapable reality of his body, its failings, its dysfunction, its eventual collapse into terminal illness. He was hypersensitive to changes in his physical condition. He was a hypochondriac. He fretted about his diet, his constitution, his need for physical exercise."

He saw Eduradova's ballet and a troupe from L'viv staging at Café Savoy in May 1910. In July 1910 he woke one Sunday, after a night of interrupted sleep, to reflect on his 'miserable life'. His self-analysis now developed a new theme, which would culminate in the famous *Letter to the Father* of 1919. This long drawn-out reproach is followed by a story, "Unhappiness," which centres on a 'bachelor' who has insufficient involvement with the world to be able to withstand its shocks. One persistent consolation throughout his life was the countryside. A thoroughly urban animal, he nevertheless loved the country and the open air. In spite of his tendency to deprecate his physical capacity, he liked to walk, kept a bicycle in his Prague flat, and enjoyed swimming at the Civilschwimmschule (Civilian Swimming School), a bathing and boating establishment moored on the opposite bank of the Vltava from the Old Town. He loved horse-riding and took lessons in sport.

Kafka then visited Saaz, and delivered a lecture at the Hotel Geling in the Bohemian town of Gablonz. Then he and

Brod went to Paris. He visited Berlin in December, where he saw Schnitzler's first play *Anatol*, and a performance of *Hamlet*.

Return to Prague, however, meant a return to the physical distractions of the family apartment, which in turn were seen as a series of further obstacles to writing. The fuss attendant on the wedding of his eldest sister, Elli, to Karl Hermann, a Christian had subsided.

Kafka struggled to keep to his regular writing schedule of eight to eleven in the evening, but work and its pressures kept intruding, forcing him to reflect that "I, so long as I am not freed of my office, am simply lost." Kafka thought writing was much a serious thing, demanding not only solitude, but also truthfulness. Issues less vital than life and death raised by the restive small businessmen of Bohemia ensured that Kafka's diary for the first two months of 1911 was punctuated by business trips to inspect factories in Friedland (where there was an ivy-shrouded castle in the snow that could have stood in for the castle in his great novel) and Reichenberg.

On 26 March 1911 Kafka attended the first of a series of theosophic lectures in Prague given by Dr Rudolf Steiner. Then he met a therapist Moriz Schnitzer who told him that he was living on wrong lines. Kafka, although occasionally prone to mock the faddish aspects of the natural therapy industry, was seriously committed to its precepts. He slept with the window open all the year round, wore light clothing, avoided meat except when medical advice insisted on it at certain periods, and drank no alcohol.

He wrote nothing during the period but had started to read about Dickens, an experience which prompted a reflection that a writer experiences a story within him, is pursued by it and entirely given over to it, wherever it may lead. In August of the year he and Brod visited Zurich, Paris and other towns. In Italy, at Osteno, he experienced a "shivery feeling at the sight of lizards wriggling on a wall" and at Menaggio reflected on the fact that "Every word of Italian spoken to one penetrates the great void of one's own ignorance." From Milan, the two friends journeyed to Paris to see the paintings of the Louvre and visit Versailles. They saw Carmen at the Opera Comique and later Racine's Phedre. Here there were sensibly conducted brothels. Kafka was impressed by the city of Paris.

On 30 September 1911 Kafka attended the Staronova synagogue in Prague for Yom Kippur, the Day of Atonement. His Jewish inheritance became another bone of contention between him and his father. In the famous *Letter to the Father* he carefully distinguished three different attitudes towards Judaism that he believed his father had implanted in him. He complained that his father did not enlighten him enough on Jewism. He went to the synagogue four times of a year. He noticed that his father was not a Jew sufficiently. He noticed that many Jews migrating to cities, lost their piety. However, Hermann began to rail against the Jewish writings his son was starting to explore, claiming that they 'nauseated' him.

Nicholas Murray speaks of another tournament for Kafka, "As if the battle between writing and work were not enough, a new source of anguish was about to torment Kafka. His brother-in-law, Elli's husband, Karl Hermann, a self-confident and worldly businessman, planned to set up a factory manufacturing asbestos, with Kafka as a joint partner. Hermann Kafka was keen to see his son-in-law prosper in business and for his son to start making money for a change, instead of all that pointless scribbling."

The appearance of the troupe of Yiddish actors from Lemberg in Galicia was a gratifying distraction for the harried Kafka. Lowy was the director and moving force behind the troupe, and he and Kafka became close friends—to the consternation of Hermann Kafka, who did not want these wild, gypsy-like Jews in his house. "Whoever lies down with dogs gets up with fleas" was the proverb that Hermann tossed at his son as his comment on this undesirable liaison. This Lowy died in a death camp of Treblinka in 1942. There is an amusing fictionalization of him in Isaac Bashevis Singer's story "A Friend of Kafka," where the narrator says of Kafka that he "wanted to be a Jew, but he didn't know how. He wanted to live, but he didn't know this either. . . He was sunk to his neck in the bourgeois swamp."

The plays of the Yiddish theatre—or *Jargontheater*—were mostly written between 1880 and 1910, and, according to one scholar, they were "immune to the revolution in modern drama at that time." It is possible that some of the characteristics of Kafka's writing—such as his reliance on gesture and exaggerated action, as well as the dark humour and comic irony—may be traced back to the overemphatic acting styles of the Lemberg troupe. It was not long after his experience of the *jargontheater* that he wrote "The Judgment," which was his first significant writing.

Unlike Hebrew, which is an ancient Semitic tongue, Yiddish is an Indo-European language that developed from medieval German and became the vernacular of the ghettoes of Eastern Europe. The social aspects of Yiddish literature appealed to Kafka. He started to read, as a supplement to Lowy's oral information, *The History of the Jews* by Heinrich Graetz.

Yet in spite of this new arrival of energy and fresh perspective in his life, the irreducible struggle to write continued. Sitting at the family table where they were playing cards he could only reflect miserably on the fact that "I lead a horrible, synthetic life... the possible happiness becomes ever more impossible." The sheer noise and bustle of the Kafka apartment were enough to prevent any serious attempts at writing. Surely the transformation in *The Metamorphosis* is gestating here. This noise and glare, probably made him aspire for a marriage. It was around this time that Kafka wrote the short piece which begins: "It seems so dreadful to be a bachelor. ..."

In June Kafka and Brod decided to take a holiday, in the course of which they would visit the Goethehaus at Weimar. The following day they left their quiet, pretty hotel, visited the Schillerhaus and then returned to the Goethehaus, where the study and bedroom struck Kafka as "sad, reminding one of dead grandfathers."

Then Kafka attended the Jungborn nature therapy in Harz mountains. Whatever the efficacy of the nature therapy, three weeks in the fresh air for the anxious, hard-worked Kafka, with no office, no family criticism, no worries about the asbestos factory, could only have been beneficial. He was reading voraciously the *Bible*, Schiller, Plato, Flaubert and keeping his usual eye out for pretty young women.

Still Kafka doubted of time and confidence for completing his novel *The Man Who Disappeared.* He said he was stabbed by the familiar writer's self-doubt. Later in 1950 the American critic Edmund Wilson said Kafka was being 'widly overdone.' He admired Kafka as a short story writer, but felt that the two most famous novels were 'rather ragged performances.' This clearly shows Kafka's modern anguish. Jorge Luis Borges is more perceptive. He said of Kafka: "One could define his work as a parable whose theme is the moral relation of the individual with God and with His incomprehensible universe."

In 1911, Rowohlt, the publisher decided to publish Kafka's first collection of stories called *Meditation.* Now Kafka read Franz Grillparzer (1791-1872), a fine playwright and novelist. Grillparzer lived a frustrated life of a bureaucrat in Vienna.

On 14 August 1911, Kafka met the beautiful Felice Beauer at Brod's house, and this lady played her own role in his life during the next five years. Interestingly, Part II of Nicholas Murray's biography of Kafka is aptly called Felice. Felice was born in Neustadt, Upper Silesia, on 18 November 1887. Her Viennese father had married the daughter of a Neustadt dyer, but in 1899 the family moved to Berlin, where her father worked for a foreign company. After leaving school in 1908, Felice went out to work to help her mother support her four brothers and sisters. She used a dictating machine known as the parlograph. She worked in Berlin. Dora Diamant quotes Kafka's words: "She was an excellent girl, but utterly bourgeois. Kafka felt that marrying her would mean marrying the whole lie that was Europe."

Nicholas Murray records an interruption in Kafka's life now. These pre-publication jitters were contributing to his failure to make any progress with *The Man Who Disappeared.* A visit at this time by Uncle Alfred from Spain further unsettled Kafka, who asked his uncle how he managed to be at one and the same time dissatisfied and yet at home everywhere. His uncle replied that, after some pointless social engagement, "I go home and regret that I didn't marry." Then his sister, Valli, announced her engagement. Marriage was in the air. But Kafka did not hear back from Felice until the end of September.

Kafka sat through entire night 22 September 1912 and wrote the story "The Judgment." It was a breakthrough. Interesting as the *Betrachtung* pieces were, the bold narrative confidence and dramatic clarity of "The Judgement" signalled a leap forward in Kafka's fictional world. He thinks seriousness is important for a writer. In his first reflection on it Kafka referred to "thoughts about Freud, of course." It is his first reference to the psychoanalyst, whose reputation was established firmly by this time, and the central importance of father-son conflict in Kafka's work generall (and in "The Judgment" in particular) might seem to sanction a classic Freudian approach to its analysis. There is something of Kafka in both Georg and in "the friend from Russia" who fails as a businessman and is resigning himself to becoming a permanent bachelor.

His later lover Milena Jesenska translated this story into Czech. At this time, his brother-in-law Karl left for 14 days business tour, forcing Kafka to look after the asbestos factory. Kafka hated this. This factory closed in 1917. The building still stands in Prague.

As the relationship developed, Kafka began to fear that he was tormenting Felice with his displays of pain, not to mention "by my existence, my very existence." A pattern began to emerge in the relationship of self-condemnation linked to compensating dependence on her, which must have seemed to Felice burdensome. Sending her a short piece, "Great Noise," which had just appeared in the Prague literary magazine *Herder-Blatter*, and which ironically represented the Kafka apartment as the headquarters of noise, he pointed out that his youngest sister Ottla, now just 20, "is my best friend in Prague, and the other two [Elli and Valli] are both sympathetic and kind. It's only my father and I who hate each other." Once he wrote, "My health is only just good enough for myself alone, not good enough for marriage, let alone fatherhood." Felice was so distressed at Kafka's anguish and madness, that she visited Max Brod to seek an explanation for his behaviour. Brod had been in Berlin and had telephoned Felice. Brod asked her to make some allowance for Kafka as he speaks of things absolutely.

Yet in spite of everything, Kafka was in love with Felice, clinging to her, wanting her, and needing her. On 23 November Kafka wrote to her: "Dearest, oh God, how I love you!"

Kafka readied the first part of *The Metamorphosis* in 1912, and read it to his friends Oskar Baum and Max Brod. Like Kafka, Gregor Samsa lives with his parents, hates the office, entertains impotent dreams of escape, and speaks softly, as if his family life has caused in him a traumatic aphasia. When Gregor is chased away by his father: "No plea of Gregor's availed, indeed none was understood; however meekly he twisted his head his father only stamped the harder." Steven Berkoff writes, "The story is characteristic of Kafka's ability to sustain a weirdly non-naturalistic situation by means of vivid particularity, a kind of hyper-realism that carries the strangeness on its back. The senses of horror, self-disgust, anguish and claustrophobia are vividly and dramatically present. And they are Kafka's emotions at this time." Steven Berkoff memorably put Gregor Samsa on the London stage in 1969 at the Roundhouse and again at the National Theatre in 1976, with later revivals around the world.

In the middle of December, not long after the publication of a review of "The Judgment" (which Kafka always referred to as 'your story' when mentioning it to Felice) in the magazine *Bohemia*, in which Paul Wiegler (who had heard the then unpublished story delivered at a public reading in Prague) called it the mark of "a great, surprisingly great talent, passionate and disciplined, which already has the strength to go its own way." In addition, the collection of stories – some of the 8 to 10 years old – *Betrachtung,* had just appeared at the end of November.

Brod met Felice in Berlin around Christmus 1912, and Felice said him. "It is very strange, we write to each other quite regularly and very often, I have had a great many letters from him, I would like to help him, but it is very difficult, he makes it very difficult for me, we never seem to get any closer." The tragedy of this relationship is inscribed here, but both would struggle on for another four years, inflicting pain and anguish on themselves, until they could do so no longer. What exactly did Kafka want? To judge from one of his letters, Felice was in the habit of saying to him: "Now, Franz, what am I to do with you?" His answer was that "you must really know me at my worst as well as at my best."

On 3 February 1913 Kafka was sent on business by the Institute to Leitmeritz for a court case. He told Felice that he would far rather have paid a visit to Berlin to see her, followed by a trip south to the French Riviera, where Max and Sophie Brod were enjoying their honeymoon. The thought of the newlyweds increased Kafka's sense of loneliness. Ottla accompanied her brother to Leitmeritz.

Kafka met Felice for the second time in March 1913. Eventually they made contact and took a walk together in the Grunewald, sitting on a tree trunk to talk. They may have visited the grave of Heinrich von Kleist.They spoke again on the hotel telephone before his departure for Leipzig, where he had a meeting with his publisher Kurt Wolff (to whom he had promised to send the manuscript of *Metamorphosis*), followed by a business trip for the Institute to Aussig.

Whether at Felice's instigation or on his own initiative, Kafka decided to try to combat his poor health, sleeplessness and generally addled spirit by trying to adopt a healthier and more active lifestyle.

On 1 May Kafka told Felice that "a very short book of mine" was to be published in June in a new young writers' series from Wolff called *The Day of Judgment*. "The Stoker," the first chapter of *The Man Who Disappeared* and "The Judgment," also appeared in this slim volume *The Sons*.

In spite of the two meetings in Berlin and the myriad ill omens, however, the couple persisted with their epistolary love affair.

A welcome respite from all this angst was provided by the arrival in Prague of Lowy, who on 2 June performed an evening of Yiddish recitations and songs, organized by Kafka at the Hotel Bristol.

In spite of all this distress, pain, uncertainty and reproach, Kafka resolved to go forward. Between 10 and 16 June he drafted a letter which would be his proposal of marriage, ten months after their first meeting, and after they had seen each other only three times.

Felice's next objection was that he might not be able to stand life with her. This was true only in the sense that he was lost to all social intercourse.

On 3 July 1913, his thirtieth birthday, Kafka finally told his mother that he was engaged. She took it with remarkable calm.

As the reality of formal engagement approached, Kafka became inflamed with anguish—"squirming before you like something poisonous,—and full of fear that marriage would turn him into a dangerous lunatic." He told Felice: "You have no idea... what havoc literature creates inside certain heads."

Apparently for the first time, he read Kierkegaard in an anthology of his writings. Like Kleist, here was another writer whose case "is very similar to mine. . . He bears me out like a friend."

Kafka wrote a letter to Felice's father Carl Bauer, quoting his qualities, selfishness, and literature as his breathing. Yet the Bauers consented to Felice's marriage with Franz. Yet Franz was worried as the marriage, he thought, might affect his writing. He knew great writers like Grillparzer, Kleist and Flaubert did not marry.

In September, Kafka went to Venice and wrote to Felice, "We shall have to part." It was a sense of failure, of exclusion from normal married life, rather than disgusted sexual recoil from its reality, that saddened him.

That difficulty, however, was real. Kafka told Brod that, though 'it is all over' and he wrote no more letters to Felice, "still, still, I cannot free myself." He repeated the mantra "I cannot live with her and I cannot live without her", adding: "I ought to be whipped out into the desert." Kafka, bereft of Felice, thought of suicide.

Grete Bloch briefly entered the post-Felice vacuum in the role of confidante by becoming the recipient of the letters Kafka could not write to Felice. She was Felice's friend to help as an intermediary. On the other hand, Kafka could not leave Felice alone. And, in spite of her declaration in Berlin that the affair was over, she was writing to him again by the middle of March. She revealed that there were problems within the Bauer family, but also, with this letter, she succeeded in reviving with a shock the former intensity of feeling between them. Truly, he could not live without her. Felice also wrote to Kafka's mother, who, having seen the distress caused by Felice's silence, had secretly urged her to reply to Kafka's letters.

Kafka persisted, in spite of a realization that, after eighteen months' running to meet each other, they were still far apart. He made his trip to Berlin on the weekend of 12-13 April 1914. While there, the engagement of Franz Kafka and Felice Bauer was finally announced. Julie Kafka immediately sent Felice losing no time in addressing her as Dear Daughter.

The prospect of marriage meant the cancellation of Kafka's plans to go to Berlin and work as a journalist, but there was no cessation of his habit of obsessive analysis of the relationship. Felice was to quit her job in August, flat-hunting began, an engagement notice appeared on 21 April in the Berliner Taghlatt, and Kafka wrote to his prospective mother-in-law (addressing her as Dear Mother) to say that, though she "may have detected certain shortcomings in me. . . none of us is perfect," and she was giving her daughter "to a man who certainly loves her no less than you do."

Once his engagement in Berlin was over Kafka wrote a short sketch, "Temptation in the Village," which points towards *The Castle,* written eight years later.

Kafka's marriage tensions continued. Even Grete worried about Felice's problem if she married Kafka. She sounded the warning bell about Kafka weakness, indecision, self-doubt and plain unsuitability for her friend. All this surfaced in a discussion at Askanischer Hof in Berlin where Julie also attended it. Grete plotted against Kafka and Felice did not like the marriage. Julie then said "Perhaps he is not made for marriage, since his only endeavour is his writing, which is the most important thing in his life."

In August 1914 the World War I began. Both Valli and Elli's husbands took part in the war. The war despaired Kafka further. He developed death wish at age 31. The passion for literature alone could not sustain his life. "I am risking nothing because my life in Prague is leading to nothing good." His practical plan was to take his savings of 5,000 kronen and live off them in Berlin or Munich.

In August 1914, Kafka began work on *The Trial*. He availed much leave for this. At this time Felice's father passed away. Now Kafka finished the novel *The Man Who Disappeared,* the stories "In the Penal Colony," "Before the Law," "The Giant Mole" and finally finished *The Trial.* The last few months of 1914 is described as the second great period in Kafka's writing.

Certainly, self-punishment was a leading theme of his writing at this time. *Der Verschollene*, the novel that is now known as *The Man Who Disappeared*, was first published in 1927, three years after Kafka's death, with Brod's title *Amerika*. The first chapter, "The Stoker" was published separately by Kurt Wolff in May 1913. The novel has rightly been called "the Cinderella among Kafka's three novels." When he offered "The Stoker" to Wolff in April 1913, Kafka suggested putting it in one volume with *The Metamorphosis* and "The Judgment" under the title *The Sons.* The reason for this suggestion is obvious: all three stories concern the fate of young men, exiled, threatened or sent to their deaths by their fathers. Kafka called his novel *The Man Who Disappeared* as Dickensian. The theme of the novel is, as ever, power and its abuses, the baffling way it plays with the life of the individual.

Writing to Kurt Wolff the following year, Kafka proposed a new collective title for his recent stories—now to include "In the Penal Colony"—to replace his earlier suggestion of *The Sons.* The new title was *Punishments*.

Kafka finished *The Trial* in 1914 again incompletely and Max Brod gave it a finish in 1925. It is perhaps this novel which is most associated in the minds of the reading public with the notion of Kafkaesque for it begins with an arbitrary and meaningless arrest, and takes its protagonist through an intricate labyrinth of futile protocols. There is a clear connection between Kafka's state of mind when he began this novel and its content. The conclusion one derives from the long tussle with Felice—and it is still not yet over—is that Kafka felt himself to be a victim, like Joseph K, of some nameless, malignant authority or Law.

In January 1915, Kafka wrote a story that he never finished called, "An Elderly Bachelor," whose resemblance in the opening pages to his creator might be said to lie in their occupation of the usual claustrophobic domestic interior.

The factory continued to wreak havoc on his writing, creating the usual situation of several stories being started then left unfinished.

Kafka and Felice met (for the first time since the Berlin catastrophe of July 1914) on the weekend of 23 and 24 January 1915, on neutral ground, at the border town of Bodenbach. Brief as the meeting was, Kafka managed to find time to read some of his recent work to Felice. When he returned to Prague, however, he had very confused and mixed feelings: "I think it is impossible for us ever to unite, but dare say so neither to her nor, at the decisive moment, to myself."

At the same time, Kafka's salary was raised and he thought of travelling with Felice to Switzerland. He visited with Ottla Vienna and Budapest. He read Gogol, Herzen, Browning, and Strindberg. On 11 September Kafka, Brod and the Prague Jewish mystic Georg Mordechai Langer went to see the so-called 'wonderrabbi' from Galicia who was holding court in Zizkov.

Kafka's publisher Wolff told him that some interesting news: the winner of the 1915 Fontane Prize, Carl Sternheim, who was a millionaire, had decided to offer the prize money to Kafka. The latter was baffled and confused by this gesture. The least materialistic of writers, Kafka did not want the money, as he had enough for his solitary needs, and accepted the gesture—itself revealing of how Kafka's literary standing was judged by his eminent contemporaries—only for the honour of taking a share in the prize rather than for the cash. Meanwhile, he thought of leaving the Institute. Felice thought of entering a sanatorium with him. Both stayed in a hotel for a week in Berlin, and he was happy. Now the two had the second engagement to marry after the war, and settle down in Berlin, of course, both pursuing independent careers.

Brod's own career was clearly taking off, with nearly 14,000 copies of his novel *Tycho Brahe* sold, but Kafka remained a special taste for the reading public. He said that the painfulness was not peculiar to his work alone, but "our times in general and my own times as well have also been painful and continue to be, and my own even more consistently than the times." This reminds us Freud's comments on the unconscious.

On 10 November 1916 Kafka travelled to Munich to take part in a literary reading at the Kunst-Salon Goltz. He read from "In the Penal Colony," and Felice came to listen to him. He also met several now-forgotten writers such as Gottfried Kolwel, Max Pulver, Eugen Mondt and Rainer Maria Rilke.

Taking advantage of his new writing-space in the little house in Alchemists' Street, Kafka wrote throughout the winter of 1916-17, in a series of notebooks scholars have christened the 'blue octavo notebooks' (today they are in the Bodleian Library at Oxford). In this period he wrote "The Coal-Scuttle-Rider" (1921), and stories such as "The Knock at the Manor-Gate," "The Great Wall of China," "The Warden of the Tomb," "The Bridge" and "The Hunter Gracchus." Not long after, Kafka sent 12 of the new stories that had been set down in the blue octavo notebooks to Martin Buber for possible publication in his Zionist periodical *Der Jude*. He told Buber that they would eventually be published in a book to be called *Responsibility* (the title had been changed to *A Country Doctor* when the book appeared in 1919). Buber took two animal stories "Jackals and Arabs" and "A Report to an Academy," which were published in the autumn.

In 1917 Kafka had the shock of haemorrhage in his lungs. This was TB. Kafka continued to see the illness as part of fate's plan for him. Brod asked Kafka to go to Switzerland for rest. Kafka approached his boss, Eugen Pfohl, to request either retirement or three months leave, in a scene he described as 'a sentimental comedy.'

Kafka felt that he could not marry Felice. He wept when he declared his refusal to her at the railway station. Brod pitied his condition. After a quarter of a million words and five years, it really was now all over.

In March 1919, little over a year later, Felice married a well-off Berlin businessman and had two children. In 1931 the family moved to Switzerland and then in 1936 to the United States, where Felice died on 15 October 1960. In 1955 she had sold the letters she had kept from Kafka to Schocken Books of New York. The correspondence—lengthy, anguished, sometimes rather hard to bear—constitutes a major document, in some sense a classic of epistolary love.

Now Kafka was happy with his sister Otla in her farm in Zurau. He aspired for the pure, the true and the immutable. The fact that the world is rarely pure, true and immutable did not dissuade him from this task. He articulated an aesthetic ambition which he would struggle, for the remaining years of his life, to fulfil. Around the middle of October, Kafka started to compose a series of short pieces that have become known as the 'Zurau aphorisms' or *Reflections on Sin, Suffering, Hope and the True Way.* His aphorisms attest to his religious faith. In aphorism '38 a man was amazed at how easily he went along the road to eternity; the fact was he was rushing along it downhill' and the fact that there is nothing but a spiritual world deprives us of hope and gives us certainty.

Nicholas Murray describes Franz Kafka's final phase of life as dominated by Milena. Kafka began to visit Otla's Zurau in snow, the description reminding us the beginning of *The Castle.* Kafka learnt of his friends Oskar and Brod's marriages in crisis. He read Kierkegaard and Buber. He thought of 'either/or.'

Kafka continued to write parables. He wrote "To My Father" and asked Kurt Wolft to include it in the book *A Country Doctor* (1919) which he thought to be his last collection to be published in his life time. The 'Father' figure gradually leads to God in Kafka's quarrel with his father.

Here in Zurau Kafka who had sympathy for the peasants wrote "Brotherhood of Poor Workers," a utopian sketch for them.

Kafka got back to his work in Prague in summer 1918. Brod met him, and the two talked of the war, and Kafka's learning of Hebrew. The war was over soon. Yet many people including Kafka were affected by the Spanish influenza. Meanwhile, the Habsburg Empire passed away in 1919 and the Austrian Emperor abdicated. Three days later the Republic of Czechoslovakia was proclaimed, with Tomas Masaryk as President. Franz Kafka was now a Czech citizen. His fluency in Czech would ensure that he would not fall victim. He kept his job at the Institute. In January 1919 the Great Powers started their peace conference at Versailles to determine the future of Europe.

With one other person Julie Wohryzek shared the veranda of the Pension Studl that January. She was the daughter of a Prague shoemaker and synagogue custodian and, on the evidence of surviving photographs, far prettier than Felice Bauer. Kafka described her to Brod as "Not Jewish and yet not not-Jewish, not German and yet not not-German, crazy about the movies, about operettas and comedies, wears face powder and veils, possesses an inexhaustible and non-stop store of the brashest Yiddish expressions, in general very ignorant, more cheerful than sad—that is about what she is like. If one wanted to classify her racially, one would have to say that she belonged to the race of shop-girls. And withal she is brave of heart, honest, unassuming—such great qualities in a person who though not without beauty is as wispy as the gnats that fly against my lamp."

Soon Kafka and Julie 'became engaged, though it seems that Kafka was more keen on marriage than she was. In November the banns were issued and a wedding was scheduled for the 2nd or 9th of that month, but it was postponed because they were having trouble finding an apartment.

In his latest doomed attempt to uproot himself from Prague, Kafka announced that he was planning to go and live in Munich early in 1920. He seemed disposed to follow the example of his publisher, Kurt Wolff, who was relocating there from Leipzig. Kafka and Julie wanted to go to Munich and live there. But a young Czech woman who liked to translate his stories into Czech, held him back.

A Country Doctor was published by Wolff in 1922.

Now he met a beautiful lady Milena Jesenska, the first non-Jewish woman with whom Kafka fell in love. Her extraordinary life story, which ended in the Nazi camp of Ravensbriick in 1944, has been told in Margarete Buber Neumann's *Milena.* Aged 25, unhappily married to the Prague writer Ernst Polak and living in Vienna as a Czech translator, Milena had led a rebellious youth in Prague and was a strong and fiery woman who was the first of Kafka's lovers truly to grasp the significance of his writing. Now his story "The Stoker" as translated by Milena appeared in Czech magazine *Kmen.*

Having to attend Ottla's marriage to Josef David at Prague Town Hall—and the wedding breakfast at which, myrtle in his buttonhole, he sat between David's two sisters—served only to intensify his desire to see himself more deeply involved with Milena: "What an easy life it will be when we are together." The more Kafka insisted on such an outcome, the more the faultline in this relationship became evident. Milena was less able to contemplate leaving her husband than Kafka imagined her to be.

On 13 December 1920 Kafka was granted a further three months' sick leave. He decided to take it at the tuberculosis sanatorium of a Mrs Jolan Forberger in Tatranske Matliare, the High Tatra mountains, in Slovakia. But he went to a sanatorium in Matlarhaza. Here Gustav Janouch, the son of his colleague, kept a record of his talks with Kafka, and he published it as *Conversation with Kafka* in 1953.

Kafka's correspondence with Milena continued. Milena was unhappy with Kafka's inability to cope with the world. She called him "a nude man with all others who are in dress." She eventually calmed down and wrote to Brad: "What his terror is I know down to the last nerve. . . In the four days he was with me [in Vienna, at the beginning of July 1920], he lost it. .

. I know for certain that no sanatorium will succeed in curing him. . . no psychic strengthening can overcome this terror [Kafka's Angst] because the terror prevents the strengthening. . . The flesh is too exposed; he cannot bear to see it." Her powerful life force had dragged Kafka into health.

Kafka met a young Hungarian doctor, Robert Klopstock, also a writer. Klopstock found Kafka's nature "all-embracing and overwhelming" yet not at all oppressive.

Now Kafka thought of retiring from service and visiting Palestine. He told Brod that he now had three wishes: to achieve "approximate recovery," to go to "a foreign land in the south" (not necessarily Palestine) and to practise "a modest handicraft." Yet he did none of them.

Kafka's stay at Matliare had not been a complete success. He had gained only eight kilos in weight during his eight-month stay and was still far from healthy. He now began to lament at his general weakness for common life. On 27 January 1922 he travelled to Spindelmuhle. He was thinking of his father again, and how he had made his son want to quit the world because he "would not let me live in it, in his world." In a biblical metaphor he saw himself as a person exiled and displaced by his father's power from his rightful homeland—"kind of wandering in the wilderness in reverse." He started to write his last novel *The Castle* in 1922.

He applied for retirement in 1922 and was assured that he would retire with a monthly pension of 1000 crowns.

Kafka quickly settled into his room at Plana, the attractive village on the River Luschnitz where Ottla, Pepa and their one-year-old daughter were already in residence. Over the next four months he would write here the remaining nine chapters of *The Castle*. It was a beautiful spot, with woods, rivers and gardens.

Kafka returned to Prague and the famous writer, Franz Werfel, paid him a visit. Around that time he wrote his first testament, his *Tintenzettel*, addressed to Brod, telling his friend to destroy everything "in the way of notebooks, manuscripts, letters, my own and other people's sketches and so on to be burned unread and to the last page, as well as all writings of mine or notes which either you may have or other people, from whom you are to beg them in my name. Letters which are not handed over to you should at least be faithfully burned by those who have them." This is both exactingly comprehensive and utterly unambiguous. Kafka at this time wanted to perform a kind of self-cancellation.

The Castle appears to be the most complex and ambitious of Kafka's three novels, yet one may still be permitted to prefer *The Trial* for its tauter, more dramatic construction. *The Castle* has often been read as a symbol of the Jew seeking acceptance in Gentile society.

For much of the winter of 1922 and into the spring of 1923, Kafka was ill and confined to bed. He wrote nothing, kept no diary. His old friend Hugo Bergmann, now professor of the Hebrew in Palestine, met him in Prague.

Nicholas Murray calls the last phase of Kafka life as "Dora," as the woman having dominated him.Kafka visited Muritz in 1923. Here he came across a lively lady, Tile Rossler, who later became a leading choreographer in Tel Aviv. Her friend Dora Diamant was quite pretty, She was 25 and he was 40. Dora recalled Kafka as "tall and slim and dark-skinned with a loping walk." He seemed lonely but considerate. Dora went on. She and Kafka soon became friends and read Hebrew together on the beach. Kafka described Dora as "a wonderful person." Dora Diamant was born in 1898 in Pabianice, near Lodi in central Poland. Her father Herschel, a learned man and a factory owner, moved the family soon after the turn of the century to Bedzin in Russian-controlled Silesia following the death of his wife in childbirth. The eldest daughter, Dora, became responsible for running the household and looking after her four siblings.

Dora did not like her father's extreme religiosity, and she ran away. She lived with Kafka for two years. She was happy with him and her vigour kept him happy. She was not aware of his literary merits, however. She later moved to Russia and was a communist. Finally she moved to England and died there in 1952.

At Schelesen a letter arrived from Carl Seelig, a Swiss publisher of luxury editions, who offered Kafka 1000 Swiss francs—a fabulous sum, especially to those who might be starting to worry about the escalating German inflation for one story. But Kafka could not give him any new story.

Kafka now left for Berlin after retirement. He was to live together with his last love Dora. Kafka was happy. Brod claimed: "I found an idyll; at last I saw my friend in good spirits; his bodily health had got worse, it is true. Yet for the time it was not even dangerous." Kafka was "on the right road, and truly happy with his life-companion in the last year of his life, which despite his frightful illness, perfected him." Kafka had always wanted to find this solid, right basis for living and would not have wished to have been seen by posterity as a prophet of existential absurdity.

Rising prices gradually put pressure on Kafka and Dora and they could not afford much else besides food. Theatres were expensive and Kafka sometimes read the newspapers in the Town Hall Square in Steglitz. They also shared together the burning of some of Kafka's work. True to his earlier expressed intentions, he now watched while Dora carried out his instructions. Not everything was destroyed, however, and after Kafka's death (unknown to Brod) Dora retained some notebooks and letters from Kafka which were eventually seized by the Nazis.

Kafka's health collapsed in January 1924. Life in Berlin became increasingly costly. An early visitor to the new Zehlendorf flat in late February was Uncle Siegfried Lowy, the doctor. He was shocked by Kafka's condition, and tried to persuade him to leave Berlin for a sanatorium.

The uncle forced Kafka back to Prague, and soon he went to a sanatorium in Wienerwald at Ortmann. During that stay in Prague in March, Kafka had written a story, "Josephine the

Songstress or the Mouse People." On 10 April he was transferred to the University Clinic of Professor Marcus Hajek in Vienna.

At some point in the stay at Kierling, possibly at the end of April, when things had not looked quite so bleak, Kafka proposed to Dora. He had been devastated by the rabbi's refusal, and in his last days fell back on the support of Dora and Klopstock. Speaking became very difficult, as did drinking, and he began to write the so-called "conversation slips." He demanded morpheme. His last words were "Yes, like that, it's all right like that."

Kafka's body was returned to Prague and buried on 11 June 1924 in the New Jewish Cemetery at Strasnice. Dora was distraught. Kafka's parents even arranged for the modest royalties of his work to be sent to her, as if she really were his wife. Hermann himself died in 1931, his wife Julie three years later. As the body was committed to the grave at four in the afternoon the sky darkened and rain fell. Around a hundred mourners were present as Kafka was buried with the Hebrew prayer for the dead. A week later a memorial service was held at the Kleine Biihne, the Little Theatre, in Prague, where more than 500 gathered to hear speeches, readings and eulogies proving that Kafka was a great writer, indeed. Obituaries appeared in the Prague newspapers, the most eloquent and penetrating written by Milena Jesenska on 6 July in *Narodni listy*.

Max Brod, truly Kafka's great friend, arranged the publication of Kafka's all writings for the benefit of the world. Himself a fine writer in his days he is forgotten today. He reminds us the fine American writer Higginson, who arranged the publication of Emily Dickinson's poetry. So Dickinson came to the limelight. On the other hand, Higginson is forgotten today. Brod began with *The Trial* in 1925, *The Castle* in 1926, and *Amerika* in 1927. English translations by Edwin and Willa Muir started to appear in 1930. One of those first, and very few, English readers of *The Castle* was Aldous Huxley who said,

"If you want to read a good book, get *The Castle* by Kafka. It makes the other German novelists, even Mann, look pretty thin and insubstantial. For me it's one of the most important books of this time.'" Kafka's other works were quickly translated into all the major European languages, but the Czechs were largely indifferent and, after 1938, the new Nazi occupiers banned his work, as the communist authorities would do after the war. The reputation of Kafka grew. Germany has considered he as one of the masters of modern German literature today. What more, Kafka is one of the best modernist writers.

2

Franz Kafka and Modernism

Modernism is a stage with reference to time in man's life. That way we are living in ever modern times and our thinking, in a sense, can be modernist. It is like the latest and the best. It can be in fact, ours. Modernism is a historically literary and artistic movement. This movement began in the 1890s and flourished upto the 1930s, and its impact can be felt throughout the rest of the twentieth century.

In the 1920s the term modernism began to be understood as experimentation in all arts. It meant progressive attitude as well. It was avant garde. *A Survey of Modernist Poetry* was first published by Laura Riding and Robert Graves in 1927, but the authors tend to use the adjective 'modern' rather than 'modernism' in most of the text of that stimulating book. And it is noticeable that neither I.A. Richards in *The Principles of Literary Criticism* (1924) nor Dr. F.R. Leavis in *New Bearings in English Poetry* (1932) employed the term 'Modernism,' although both were concerned with 'modern' qualities in poetry, especially that of T.S. Eliot–"a modern sensibility" as Leavis called him. Yet the movement could not have a name. Graham Hough in *Image and Experience* in 1960 found the same difficulty of terminiology: "The years between 1910 and the Second World War saw a revolution in the literature of the English language as momentous as the Romantic one of a century before..... (but it) has not yet acquired a name." Hough's suggestion was to extend the term Imagism: Imagist ideas are at the centre of the characteristic poetic procedures of our time, and there is a case for giving the word a wider connotation. *The Pelican Guide to English Literature* (1961) used the term modernism. Bernard Bergonzi's essay "The Coming of Modernism" (1971) discusses this phenomenon.

However, there is inexactness about the use of the concept "modernism." This chapter treats the so called European modernism with reference to such great writers/thinkers as that of Sigmund Freud, Karl Marx, Franz Kafka, Joseph Conrad, James Joyce, W.B. Yeats, Henry James, Ezra Pound, T.S. Eliot, Virginia Woolf, D.H. Lawrence, Gertrude Stein, William Faulkner, Ernest Hemingway, Marianne Moore and others.

What is true of Romanticism as a reaction to Neo-Classicism, is also true of modernism which is a reaction to Victorian Age in Europe. Modernism is a part of the historical and reactionary process by which the arts have disassociated themselves from the nineteenth century assumptions which were then dead assumptions.

The most obvious concern is with realism in literature. This is more particularly in fiction. The Victorian novelists followed the path left by Jane Austen as suggested by Scott: "The art of copying from nature as she really exists in the common walks of life, and presenting to the reader instead of the splendid scenes of an imaginary world, a correct and striking representation of that which is daily taking place around him." This emphasis on common experience is typical of the Victorian novelists – of Thackeray, Trollope, Mrs. Gaskell and George Elliot. Thackeray, indeed, complained of Dickens's failure in this respect in a letter to David Masson in 1851; "I quarrel with his Art in many respects: which I don't think represents Nature duly."

Peter Faulkner observes, "That consensus, the view that writer and reader share a justified expectation of what literature is and can provide, did not need to be confined to the realistic novel. With the drama it simply took the form of the belief that entertainment was paramount, in burlesque, melodrama, pantomime – or, indeed, Shakespeare. In poetry as in the novel, the expectation was of ethical enlightenment, to be conveyed in a form intelligible to a wide audience. It was because Tennyson was prepared to fulfill these requirements that he came to occupy so prominent a position in the intellectual life of his time." Tennyson spoke for and to his age, and the *Idylls of the King* themselves were written as his fullest effort to express sound moral teaching in the form of poetry. "It was because Tennyson came to accept this 'public' conception of poetry that he was able to fulfil the duties of Poet Laureate with such confidence and was perhaps the last poet so able to act. In other Victorian poets such as Browning and Hopkins there is a gap between the poetry and the audience's expectations. All that is of true and lasting worth in poetry, must have its root in a sound view of human life and the condition of man in the world. *In Memorian* was the poem in which Tennyson managed to fulfil these expectations while at the same time expressing his own deep perplexities. In his later poems, it sometimes seems as if his sense of public responsibility plays too large a part in determining the nature of what he writes.

In England the reaction came later with the Pre-Raphaelitism of Rossetti and Swinburne denounced so vituperatively by Robert Buchanan as "The Fleshy School of Poetry" in 1871. In Oscar Wilde's formulation in "The Decay of Lying" in 1890 the whole Victorian position is nearly subverted. "The Final revelation is that lying, the telling of beautiful untrue things, is the proper aim of Art." Thus the moral earnestness of the mid-century was finally dissipated in the extravagances and paradoxes of the Nineties.

The Pre-Raphaelities and Aesthetes challenged the Victorian orthodoxies. Bernard Shaw reacted to the Romantic drama as Hardy and George. Moore reacted to the Victorian fiction. The outraged reception of Hardy's *Jude the Obscure* (1896) shows the shock caused when a novelist tried to alter the focus of the novel. The Bishop of Wakefield wrote to the *Yorkshire Post* to relate that he had been so disgusted with its insolence and indecency that he threw it on the fire. Hardy's dignified remark in his 1902 Preface that he could see nothing exceptionable in his handling of the tragic theme in "a novel addressed by a man to men and women of full age" suggests his sense that the novel should belong not to the Victorian family fireside but to the mature and responsible reader.

This suggests the breakdown of artistic, ethical and social assumptions.

If Hardy gave up novel for poetry, Henry James devised new theories of the art of fiction. He wrote "The Art of Fiction" in 1884. James argued indeed, that theoretical understanding, such as he found in the French novelists from Flaubert to Zola, was necessary to complete artistic success, and himself provided, in his many reviews and in the Prefaces he wrote for the New York edition of his novels (1906-7), the most sustained criticism of the novel in English.

Here James is applying the language of the Romantic critics, especially Coleridge, to the novel. The concern with organic unity remained central for him, and led him away later from Victorian conventions. But he always argued that unity did not mean simply selectıng a limited range of materials; on the contrary, fiction was animated by the attempt to catch "the note and trick, the strange irregular rhythm of life." James is critical of the conventional novel, and advocates a deeper kind of unity as his ideal. The idea of unity, of organic form, is central to James's thinking about the novel. But he does not seek this unity in what might seem the simplest way: by writing only short novels, or stories on single subjects. What he values about the novel is certainly not its exclusiveness; he often emphasizes its variety as a merit.

This was to be his method in such large-scale novels as *The Portrait of a Lady* and *The Ambassador*. But in *The Golden Bowl* (190) James went further, giving the first part of the novel to the Prince and the second to the Princess.

Nor was this problem in fact confined to the novel. An attempt to answer it can be seen also in the poetry and criticism of W.B. Yeats another transitional figure, who began to publish while Tennyson was still Poet Laureate and who was writing poetry up to his death in 1939. But the aesthetic or symbolist position did not satisfy Yeats for long. He began to sense that the rejection of Victorian rhetoric and externalities was leading to a poetry whose purity was anaemic. In "In the Seven Woods" (1903), "The Great Helmet" (1910) and "Responsibilities" (1914),

Yeats began to create a new kind of poetry in accordance with his changed views.

Although Yeats presents the choice as open, his own sympathy Is clearly with the literature represented by Villon. He believes that poetry should be an integrated art, the expression of the whole personality, "blood, imagination, intellect, running together." The Symbolists followed the Romantics in their devotion to the imagination; the Victorians, it might be argued, cultivated some forms of intellect; but that elemental force, the blood, had appealed to neither. From this point onward in his career Yeats is always striving to create a poetry with this power of integration, though always aware of the forces in the modern world making for incoherence and confusion. In the volumes which he published during the era of modernism, and especially in *The Tower* (1928), he attempted to solve the problem of the tension between the awareness of complexity and the commitment to unity. The modernism of the later Yeats shows itself partly in his concern for such a balance between pattern and experience.

Peter Faulkner observes this about the era of modernism: "1910-1930:" "Socially the period was one of widespread turmoil and suffering, including the 1914-18 war and the beginning of the economic depression. Yet culturally it was a great creative period, which produced such works as Eliot's *The Waste Land,* Pound's *Hugh Selwyn Mauberley,* Joyce's *Ulysses,* Lawrence's *Women in Love,* Virginia Woolf's *To the Lighthouse,* and Yeats *The Tower*, to say nothing of the contemporary work of Rilke, Blok, Mayakovsky, Pasternak, Machado, Apollinaire, Ungaretti, Alberti, Mann, Proust, Kafka, and Svevo. And this is in literature alone. The challenge to the artist is always to combine openness to experience with formal control, and the art of this troubled period often thrived on the challenge." The beginning of the twentieth century witnessed a massive struggle in all walks of European life.

Politically and economically, the labour movements captured power against the capitalists. Socially speaking the feminists grew much more strong. Accepting one's place, loyalty to authority, unquestioning obedience, began to break down;

patriotism, doing one's duty, even Christianity, seemed questionable ideals. Man's understanding himself was changing. Anthropology was probing the primitive roots of religion: James Frazer's *The Golden Bough* appeared in 12 volumes between 1890 and 1915. Philosophers like Nietzsche and Bergson had already emphasized the importance of instinct rather than reason, psychologists like Freud and Jung were showing the power and significance of the unconscious. Scientific explanations were becoming more subtle and harder for the laymen to understand.

The twentieth century artist and writer saw himself confronted by the infinite complexity of realities. In his book *The Struggle of the Modern* in 1953, Stephen Spender said, "Modern art is that in which the artist reflects awareness of an unprecedented modern situation in form and idiom, and second that the principle of reality in our time is peculiarly difficult to grasp and that 'realism'" is not an adequate approach to it. The same point emerges in Eric Auerbach's wide ranging study of the representation of reality in Western literature. Auerbach considers a great variety of methods from Homer onwards, and his last chapter, entitled 'The Brown Stocking', focuses on Mrs. Ramsay in Virginia Woolf's *To the Lighthouse*."

Similarly, in Joyce's *Ulysses,* Auerbach notes the "dizzying whirl of motifs, wealth of words and concepts, perpetual playing on their countless associations, and the ever re-aroused but never satisfied doubt as to what order is ultimately hidden behind so much apparent arbitrariness." The sense of the almost overwhelming abundance of the experience to be made into art marks off modernism from the rarefied atmosphere of symbolism and aestheticism. Experimentation characterizes modernism in all its spheres. The artists found out new methods of organization, particularly through juxtaposition (rather than simple narrative) and irony (rather than unity of mood).

Joseph Frank's important article "Spatial Form in Modern Literature" in 1945 discussed the decline of chronological narrative structures in modern literature, and its replacement by what he called "spatial form," the presentation of the unity of a work in "the entire pattern of internal references," or "the principle of reflexive references." This method Frank found common to *The Waste land, The Cantos, Ulysses,* Proust, and Djuna Barnes's *Nightwood.* The reader is being asked not to follow a story but to discern a pattern.

For some readers and critics this has been the central weakness of Modernism. In its pursuit of a more complex sense of reality, it is felt to have failed in coherence. This is an issue that has been constantly and indeed relevantly raised throughout the history of modernism.

The use of myth is one way in which the modernist writer has felt able to give coherence to his work, the myths often being of the most general kind, concerned with death and regeneration, the cycle of nature, the order of the seasons, though sometimes, as in the case of *Ulysses,* more specifically literary. But there are other ways of achieving unity in modernist works. For example, an analogy with music was used by I.A. Richards.

The modernists went on to contrast the essential unity of *The Waste Land* with the adventitious unity of *In Memoriam* and ascribed simply a metrical regularity. A parallel contrast was made by Herbert Read in *Form in Modern Poetry* in 1932, contrasting 'organic' with 'abstract' from. Modernist literature has its own kind of order which is subtle, complex and satisfying.

One characteristic of Modernism, then, is an acute awareness of the problems of art, an unremitting self-consciousness. Magazines played a very important part in making the new ideas about art current in the intellectual life of the time. They included A. R. Crage's *New Age,* Ford Madox Ford's *English Review,* Richard Aldington's *Egoist,* Ezra Pound and Wyndham Lewis's *Blast* and later Lewis's *Enemy,* Edgell Rickword's *Calendar of Modern Letters,* Middleton Murry's *Athenaeum* and later his *Adelphi,* Eliot's *Criterion* and F.R. Leavis's *Scrutiny.* Unlike their Victorian predecessors, many of them were short lived. But as their function, too, was different to introduce new work and new ideas about art rather than to apply accepted standards they can be seen as influential to different degrees. Important volume of criticism were also published, often drawing on material from the magazines. This criticism included Eliot's *The Sacred Wood* (1920), Percy Lubbock's *Craft of Fiction* (1921), Murry's *Problem of Style* (1922), T.E. Hulme's *Speculations* edited by Herbert Read (1924), I.A. Richard's *Principles of Literary Criticism* (1924), Eliot's *Homage to John Dryden* (1924), Virginia Woolf's *The Common Reader* (1925), Edwin Muir's *Transition* (1926), Laura Riding and Robert Graves's *Survey of Modernist Poetry* (1927), E.M. Forster's *Aspects of the Novel* (1927), Eliot's *For Lancelot Andrewes* (1928), Richard's *Practical Criticism* (1929), Muir's *Structure of the Novel* (1929), William Empson's *Seven Types of Ambiguity* (1930), Wilson Knight's *Wheel of Fire* (1930) and *The Imperial Theme (*1931*)*. Edmund Wilson's *Axel's Castle* (1931) and Leavis's *New Bearings in English Poetry* (1932).

The characteristic demand of modernism arose from the writers' sense of the difficulty of their task. Only a complex and demanding art, it was felt, could adequately render a modern consciousness of the world. This feeling can be accounted for in several ways. It can be said that all great art is complex. The modern world is more complex than previous forms of society, owing to the effects of a technology which has not only filled the world with more 'things' than ever before but also changed the relatively settled relationships of the feudal era for the confused openness of the modern industrial state.

It is in poetry and the novel that modernism can first be most clearly discerned. At least in English and American literature, on which this account is focused, developments in drama followed a different course. The influence on Bernard Shaw certainly moved drama away from some nineteenth century conventions, but the methods which he used instead were consistent with a rationalistic philosophy. The more radical innovations of the later Ibsen, and of Strindberg and Pirandello, had no immediate influence in England. Brecht's combination of technical innovation with a strong political and moral emphasis was more readily accepted in the thirties, but led to no major work. His insistence on the "alienation effect" in order to force the audience into judgment rather than identification paralleled the modernist repudiation of simple responses, but was far more definite and conclusive in intention. The post-1945 work of Arthur Miller and Tennessee Williams in America, and later of John Osborne and Arnold Wesker in England, also tended towards the direct representation of social experience rather than the complexities of Modernism. Only with the plays of Samuel Beckett and Eugene Ionesco, followed creatively by Harold Pinter, did the drama take a form recognizably modernist. But because of the dates of these developments and their parallels in the other arts it might be argued in terms that drama has a less significant palaeo-modernist phase, and a more significant neo-modernist one. The reasons for this must remain debatable, but the social nature of the theatre as an institution must be among them.

The acceptance of a modernist view of poetry in England was certainly accelerated by the influence of Eliot's early criticism, the restrained and elegant manner of which could persuade readers who rejected Ezra Pound's more polemical assertion of similar attitudes. Eliot's volume of essays *The Sacred Wood* appeared in 1920, two years before the best known and most discussed of modernist poems, *The Waste Land,* so that the bases of the new poetic were asserted early. And the central concern of *The Sacred Wood,* was, as Eliot put it in his Preface to the 1928 edition "the problem of the integrity of poetry," to show the essential nature of poetry as distinguished from other forms of knowledge or discourse. In doing this, Eliot found it necessary to re-define the nature of criticism.

Modernism flourished even after the 1930s. The Worldwide economic depression was disastrous. The eruption of Fascism and Nazism in Italy and Germany led to the Great World War II. What the American Marxist critic Edmund Wilson says is that modernist writers did not write with a politics that would avoid wars. The post-1930 or the new generation writer was much more political, generally left-wing. Especially in poetry, direct criticism of English society became frequent. Michael Roberts in the preface to his anthology *New Signatures* in 1932, which included poems by W.H. Auden. C. Day Lewis, William

Plomer and Stephen Spender, wrote of poetry being "turned to propaganda," and Day Lewis in *A Hope for Poetry* (1934) and Louis MacNeice in *Modern Poetry* (1937) criticized the lack of political concern in the poets of the previous generation. George Orwell took care of politics in his *1984* (1949) and *Animal Farm* (1945). Other examples are Sartre, Camus, Pasternak, Solzhenitsyn, Baldwin and Mailor.

Post 1930 western criticism is also reactionary to Modernism. Yvor writers said that modernism was not inclusive. In England, related critical attitudes found their expression in the fifties, especially in the group of writers associated with Robert Conquest's anthology *New Lines* (1956). A little earlier, one of the poets represented in the anthology, Donald Davie, had published *Purity of Diction in English Verse* (1952), in which he tried to explain the pleasure to be found in the non-metaphorical verse of the eighteenth century. Reservations about Modernism are characteristic too of Marxist criticism, despite the burst of artistic experimentation in the Soviet Union in the years immediately after the Revolution (1917), including the work of Mayakovsky, Blok, Pasternak and Mandelstam. The Stalinist period included an assault on formalism and the establishment of the unyielding orthodoxy of Socialist Realism. Non-Russian Marxists took less rigorous lines, and their concern for society and the wide dissemination of ideas made them wary of Modernism.

The Hungarian critic George Lukacs argued that Modernist writers fail to see man socially and historically, and so make his alienation, which is a social process, into an absolute. They offer a totally subjective vision, leading to "the attenuation of reality" in Joyce Kafka, Musil, Faulkner and Beckett inevitably accompanied by dissolution of personality. Tellingly, Lukacs suggests that Kafka replacs the world by his angst ridden vision of the world. This argument assumes the very condition the modernists question – that 'the world' is objectively real. Kafka's *angst* is seen as "the experience *par excellence* of modernism," which finally means "not the enrichment by the negation of art." This view is reaffirmed in an essay on "Franz Kafka or Thomas Mann." Although non-Marxist critics may be more eclectic than Lukacs, they often express a view of the limitations of modernism which is indebted to his account.

Frank Kermode's *Romantic Image* (1957) argued that the idea of a dissociation of sensibility was a misleading myth shoring up the Romantic and modernist view that the image was the central element in poetry, and suggested that 'discourse' too had an important part to play.

Literary historians were thus beginning to see the development of the century in a new pattern. A. Alvarez in *The Shaping Spirit* (1958) argued that "Modernism ... has been predominantly an American concern," because it was the American poets who needed to establish a poetic manner. English poets like Lawrence and Auden, it was suggested, were not so systematic. A similar view was presented by Graham Hough in *Image and Experience* (1960).

Great critics Stephen Spender, Harry Levin, Lionel Trilling made an analytical study of modernism. Modernism, that is to say, has not supplanted other ways of experiencing the world, nor other forms of art. A comparable point of view may be discerned in the conclusion to Michael Hamburger's *The Truth of Poetry* (1969), where he talks of the paradoxical relationship between beauty and truth and fiction and reality. Modernism was one ambitious and partly successful attempt to cope with this paradox; in its great works, the fictions are intensely human. Modernism has thus permanently enriched our literature. Though leaving its problems unresolved it has sharpened and intensified our awareness of the complexity of existence and so our need of a unifying philosophy.

Modernism has come to seem a broadly homogeneous movement, with roots in Romanticism and a flowering in the first third of the century. This recognition has been accompanied by some stringent criticisms especially from Marxist critics like Lukacs and Craig, and from critics with a particular view of the English creative tradition, like Hough and Davie. At the same time Modernism has been vigorously defended, particularly in America and France. New forms of experimentation have developed, particularly since 1950, in the works of Beckett, Burroughs, Borges, Butor, Robbe-Grillet, in forms of concrete poetry and electronic music, in the mixing of media and the increasing application of sophisticated technology in graphic arts. These developments raise questions of terminology. Is all this to be seen and described as an extension and continuation of modernism, or is it a new movement which needs a new name?

This new movement is Post-Modernism. Kermode called it 'palaeo-modernism' and 'neo modernism.'

3

Franz Kafka's Novels

Franz Kafka was a great modernist novelist and short story writer. In fact, his ideas have served greatly for literary modernism. Kafka's novels *America, The Trial, Castle* and *The Metamorphosis* are critically analyzed in the present chapter.

America (The Man Who Disappeared)

Franz Kafka's first novel *The Man Who Disappeared* (written between 1911 and 1914), otherwise known as *America* (*ka*) as Max Brod named it, was not finished by Kafta. Max Brod who knew the end of the story by Kafka, used his notes to complete it adequately. Kafka wrote it typically. He wanted to model it on Charles Dickens's *David Copperfield.* The novel is in picaresque vein, yet quite cheerful, unlike his other novels *The Trial* and *The Castle. America,* yet contains a conflict, a struggle. Michael Hofmann comments: "There is an opposing reading of *The Man Who Disappeared...* that, far from being a jolly picaresque or Chaplinade, its events actually describe a pitiless descent through American society, towards a probable catastrophe every bit as grim and ineluctable as those in *The Trial* or *The Castle."*

Anne Fuchs thinks Kafka's *The Man Who Disappeared* is set against the realist backdrop of the most modern and technologically advanced society in the world, the USA. The America of this novel remains strangely hyper-real, however, in spite of Kafka's careful depiction of various icons of modernity.

America begins with its young protagonist Karl Rossman's arriving to New York. He is sent by his parents under duress as he impregnated a maid. It is said Kafka's cousin Robert Kafka, was seduced by a family cook at the age of fourteen. This autobiographical data stars in this incident of Karl's seduction of a maid.

America is said to have been planned in childhood, concerned a quarrel between two brothers, one of whom went to America, while the other remained in prison in Europe.

In 1911 Kafka notes in his diary a remark of Edison's about the renewed energies discovered by Czech immigrants to the United States: perhaps he saw America still a land of promise for his own country men, a symbol of release from the normal conditions of his existence.

The first chapter "The Stoker" appeared in May 1913, as part of a new magazine, *Der jungste Tag*, and had several enthusiastic reviews. As a story it is straightforward: a simple account of how Karl Rossmann, an emigre from Hamburg, goes between decks after his liner arrives in New York, meets a giant stoker, defends him against a shipmate before a tribunal of the captain and his officers, and is finally recognised by a wealthy uncle who takes him ashore to his own lodging. The originality is in the mode of narration, which, like "The Judgment," slips easily from the real world into one on the borderline between reality and dreams.

America begins in a romantic vein: "As Karl Rossmann, a poor boy of sixteen who had been packed off to America by his parents because a servant girl had seduced him and got herself with child by him, stood on the liner slowly entering the harbour of New York, a sudden burst of sunshine seemed to illumine the Statue of Liberty, so that he saw it in a new light, although he had sighted it long before. The arm with the sword rose up as if it newly stretched aloft, and round the figure blew the free winds of heaven."

Karl is acquainted to a passenger and when both walk to go away from the harbour, he remembers his umbrella which he has forgotten in the ship. Soon he keeps the box to the charge of the acquaintance and rushes to the ship for his box. He befriends the stoker of the ship and he forgets his box.

He reminds us Yank, the stoker hero of Eugene O'Neil's impressionistic play *The Hairy Ape.* The stoker is in a bad shape.

Karl thinks of the stoker's helplessness: Karl loses his box as well as umbrella. He remembers his parents gave him a piece of Veronese Salami as an extra bit. Karl remembers that a Slovak in the voyage wanted to steal his box night time. Now it is confirmed as true.

The stoker meanwhile meets the members of the kitchen, and shows a kind of concern for a girl called Lina. Kafka describes the ship at the New York harbour. The waves dash to it often as if in a continual fight.

The stoker turns his eyes on Karl as if Karl were his heart, to whom he was silently bewailing his grief.

Karl on behalf of the stoker friend enquires the Head Purser and later the captain for justice: "'May I be allowed to say that in my opinion an injustice has been done to my friend the stoker? There's a certain man Schubal aboard who bullies him. He has a long record of satisfactory service on many ships, whose names he can give you, he is diligent, takes an interest in his work, and it's really hard to see why on this particular ship, where the work isn't so heavy as on cargo boats, for instance, he should get so little credit. It must be sheer slander that keeps him back and robs him of the recognition that should certainly be his."

Karl supports the stoker's case against Schubal, a Romanian, and the ship is of the Germans.

Now the Captain is attracted to Karl and asks for his name. Karl, who thinks that his main business is best served by satisfying his stubborn questioner as quickly as possible, replies briefly, without, as was his custom, introducing himself by means of his passport, which he would have had to tug out of his pocket: 'Karl Rossmann.'

"But really!" said the gentleman who had been addressed as Jacob, recoiling with an almost incredulous smile. The

Captain too, the Head Purser, the ship's officer, even the attendant, all show an excessive astonishment on hearing Karl's name. Only the Harbour Officials and Schubal remains indifferent.

"But really!" repeated Jacob, walking a little stiffly up to Karl, "then I'm your Uncle Jacob and you're my own dear nephew. I suspected it all the time!' he says to the Captain before embracing and kissing Karl, who dumbly submits to everything" (p. 219).

It is Senator Edward Jacob who just declares himself to be Karl's uncle. Karl has now a brilliant career in front of him, against all his previous expectations.

"I certainly have an Uncle Jacob in America," said Karl, turning to the Captain, "but if I understand rightly, Jacob is only the surname of this gentleman."

"That is so," said the Captain, encouragingly.

"Well, my Uncle Jacob, who is my mother's brother, had Jacob for a Christian name, but his surname must of course be the same as my mother's, whose maiden name was Bendelmayer."

Jacob received a letter from Karl's lover Johanna Brummer, a person of round about thirty-five, a maid servant in Karl's neighourhood. Jacob explains even to the Captain of the ship of Karl's seduction of Brummer, and his emigration to America. Both the stoker and Schubal as well as the other crew, listen to the story of seducation as if an adventure. The first to express his sympathy, after the Captain, is curiously enough the stoker. "I congratulate you heartily," he says.

All the while, the stoker's skirmish with Schubal continues.

Chapter 2 is entitled "Uncle Jacob." It begins thus: "In his uncle's house Karl soon became used to his new circumstances. But, indeed, his uncle indulged his slightest wishes and Karl had never to learn by hard experience, which so much embitters one's first acquaintance with foreign countries."

Karl's room is on the sixth floor of a house whose five other floors, along with three more in the basement, are taken up by his uncle's business. It is so light what with its two windows and a door opening on a balcony, that Karl is filled with fresh astonishment every morning. Where might he not have had to stay, if he had landed in this country as a destitute little emigrant? Indeed, as his uncle, with his knowledge of the emigration laws, though highly probable, Karl might not have been admitted into the United States at all and might have been sent home again without regard to the fact that he no longer had a home. Because he had no visa. In this country sympathy is something one could not hope for; in that respect America resembled what Karl had read about it; except that those who are fortunate seemed really to enjoy their good fortune here, sunning themselves among their carefree friends.

Cautious in all things, Uncle Jacob advises Karl for the time being to take up nothing seriously. He should certainly examine and consider everything, but without committing himself. The first days of a European in America might be likened to a rebirth.

However, it is by no means the sole pleasure that Karl has. In his room stands an American writing-desk of superior construction, such as his father had coveted for years and tried to pick up cheaply at all kinds of auction sales without ever purchasing one. Karl also gets a costly piano just for asking it. Even Jacob asks Karl to learn violin and the French horn as well.

The learning of English is naturally Karl's first and most important task. Mack, a young teacher from a neighbouring commercial college appears in his room every morning at seven and finds him already over his exercise books at the desk, or walking up and down the room committing words to memory. Karl wants to make rapid progress.

The better Karl's English becomes, the greater inclination his uncle shows to introduce him to his friends, arranging only that on such occasions the English teacher should always be at his elbow. With the unconditional approval of Uncle Jacob, it is arranged that this young man, whose name is Mr Mack, should take Karl out riding every morning at half-past five, either in the riding-school or in the open air. Karl needs to learn horse-riding now.

It takes a relatively long time before Uncle Jacob consents to allow Karl even the slightest insight into his business, although Karl often begs him to do so. Jacob's is a sort of commission and dispatch agency such as, to the best of Karl's knowledge, is probably not to be found in Europe.

Karl wonders at Jacob's business network. The infrastructure such as telephone office is so huge as though larger than what he could see in his village in Germany. It symbolizes Jacob's prosperity. Now Jacob begins his rag-to-riches story. "And let me tell you I started it all myself thirty years ago. I had a little business at that time near the docks and if five crates came up for unloading in one day I thought it a great day and went home swelling with pride. Today my warehouses cover the third largest area in the port and my old store is the restaurant and storeroom for my sixty-fifth group of porters."

One day his uncle appears just before dinner, which Karl had expected to take alone as usual, and asks him to put on his black suit at once and join him for dinner, together with two of his business friends. In his uncle's diningroom, which he can still remember from the evening of his arrival, two tall, stout gentlemen rise to their feet, one of them called Green, the other Pollunder.

The very next day Pollunder takes Karl to his country house as his daughter Clara is eager to see him. This is much against Jacob's wishes.

Chapter 3, "A Country House Near New York", is about Karl's visit to Pollunder's house. Kafka describes New York, its suburbs and Pollunder's country house.

No sooner do the two—Pollunder and Karl— reach the villa, than they notice Mr. Green's arrival at Pollundr's house. Green is also a businessman. He behaves indifferently with Karl. Pollunder too does not like him at this time. Karl is yet happy to see the beautiful country house. His impression of Clara is that she is beautiful, yet very assertive. Clara likes Karl's piano music.

Karl examines all the things at Pollunder's house, his daughter and Mr. Green. There are many servants. One servant surprises Karl when he says his English teacher Mack is Clara's lover. So Karl could not think of her as his lover. Lately he is much intrigued by the house. He worries much about his uncle, and this new house frightens him. And once he has put the worst into words, all the rest comes blurring out after it, and he says without the slightest insincerity things of which he has never even thought before. "I want above all to get home. I'll be glad to come again, for wherever you are, Mr Pollunder, I'll always be glad to stay. Only tonight I can't stay here. You know that my uncle was unwilling to give me permission for this visit. Until my English studies are finished and while I am still insufficiently versed in practical things, I am entirely dependent on my uncle's kindness, which I can accept, of course, being a relation. You mustn't think that I'm in a position yet to earn my living decently—and God forbid that I should do it in any other way. I'm afraid my education has been too impractical for that. I managed to scrape through four classes of a European High School with moderate success, and for earning a livelihood that means less than nothing, for our schools are very much behind the times in their teaching methods. You would laugh if I were to tell you the kind of things I learned. If a boy can go on studying, finish his school course and enter the university, then, probably, it all straightens out in the long run and he finishes up with a proper education that lets him do something and gives him the confidence to set about earning a living. But unluckily I was torn right out of that systematic course of study. Sometimes I think I know nothing, and in any case the best of my knowledge wouldn't be adequate for America."

Karl is much agitated because he came to Pollunder's house much against Jacob's liking. So he decides to go back even in the night. Now he meets Clara, and plays piano, and learns that his English master Mack is her lover.

Karl's new life in America is beset by many starting troubles.

Once Karl is out to go home by train at night, Green shocks him by conveying Jacob's message that Karl should forget his uncle just to have disobeyed him. His box and umbrella are submitted to Karl, which however, surprises him, because he had thought that he had missed them. We need to remember that Jacob had got them for Karl at the harbour. Karl's two months stay at Jacob's house and his American dream is over.

Green suggets Karl that he should go to San Francisco for job. He cannot get one in New York because his uncle has a hand in everything. In fact, he gives him a third class ticket for San Francisco.

Karl could not detect any malice in these words; the bad news which had lain sheathed in Green the whole evening is delivered, and now he seems a harmless man with whom one could speak more frankly perhaps, than with anybody else. The best of men, chosen through no fault of his own to be the bearer of such a secret and painful message, must appear a suspicious character so long as he has to keep it to himself.

Annie Fichs thinks authority and power are exercised in the novel. She observes, "Tracing Karl's odyssey through a space which is neither real nor wholly imaginary, I will argue that the novel exposes the power play of a social order which relies entirely on mechanisms of exclusion for its sense of identity."

Chapter 4, "The Road to Rameses", describes Karl's restarting of life in America. This is quite interesting as much as ironic. He reaches an inn quickly and asks for a cheap lodge. The landlord beckons him to his attic. Karl notices two young men lying there carelessly. He finds there neither a couch nor a sofa. He is as unsafe there as on the open road.

Karl opens his box and he is happy to find out whatever he had from his parents. The coat has his passport as well as money. When he examines them, the two poor sleepers get up.

Karl resolves to take every advantage of their momentary weakness and so he says: "My name is Karl Rossmann and I am a German. Please tell me, as we are occupying the same room, what your names are and what country you come from. I may as well say that I don't expect a share of your beds, for I was late in arriving and in any case I have no intention of sleeping. And you mustn't draw the wrong conclusions from the good suit I have on; I am quite poor and without any prospects."

The smaller of the two men; the one with his boots on indicating by his arms, legs and general demeanour that he is not interested in all this and has no time for such remarks, lies down again and immediately goes to sleep; the other, a dark-skinned man, also lies down again, but before falling asleep says with a languid wave of the hand: "That chap there is called Robinson, and he's an Irishman, I'm called Delamarche and I'm a Frenchman, and now please be quiet." Scarcely has he said this when with a great puff he blows out Karl's candle and falls back on the bed.

"Well, that danger is averted for the moment," Karl says himself, turning back to the table. If their sleepiness is not a pretext, everything is all right.

Yet Karl is a little uneasy about the Irishman.

Karl opens the family album and scrutinizes his parents' photos. His father looks a small and uninteresting figure. The mother looks as if in smile. He remembers his father's word that he should write them about his life in America. Karl wonders what he has to write in this bad shape. His father once exclaimed to his mother that Karl would find a good job in two months. Alas! Karl is still directionless in a garret of eating place in America. He falls asleep now.

Karl is wakened by the Frenchman in the morning. Now the two tell Karl that they are mechanics and they are on their way to Butterford for work. They ask Karl to join them.

As a parting gesture, the Irishman flings the can on the stone flags. Observed by no one, they leaves the house and step out into the thick, yellowish morning mist. They walk on in silence side by side at the edge of the road; Karl has to carry his box, since the others are not likely to relieve him unless he asks them. They notice much traffic.

There are no pedestrians, no market women straggling singly along the road towards the town, as in Karl's country, but every now and then appear great, flat motor-trucks, on which stand some twenty women with baskets on their backs, perhaps market women after all, craning their necks to oversee the traffic in their impatience for a quicker journey. There are similar trucks on which a few men loung about with their hands in their trouser pockets. These trucks bear different inscriptions. One reads: "Dock labourers wanted by the Jacob Despatch Agency." The truck happens to be going rather slowly and a lively little stoop shouldered man standing on the step invites the three wanderers to hop in.

The threesome do not like to serve Jacob's Despatch Agency as they know the ill-reputation of it. They stop at a place and Delamarche and Robinson eat Karl's Veronese salamis without giving any of it to him. Robinson carries Karl's heavy box sometimes.

Soon Karl remembers his home and thinks that he should better stay in New York. This is to help him to return home if he likes. But his two companions assure him the prospects of work in Butterford. They sight New York City, Brooklyn Bridge and the East River. Karl is happy about it. The other two wonder as to how Karl could not see New York though he stayed there for two months. Karl now knows the location where Jacob's Despatch Agency lies. Now they eat at an ordinary hotel and drink a cheap black liquor. They have a bad time to pay the bill. Neither Delamarche or Robinson has any money, though both relish the food. Karl pays it.

The three start their forward journey in the countryside. A few hours later, they reach a shady haunt and decide to stay the night there. The two elders ask Karl to buy bacon, bread and beer from the "Hotel Occidental" nearby in the town of Rameses.

Karl does it. He befriends the Manageress of the hotel as well. The woman is kindness-incarnate. She offers him and his friends free lodge. But because of Robinson's uncleanness and Delamarche's bad character, Karl refuses the help.

Once Karl comes back he notices his box is opened by Delamarche. In fact, the Frenchman is ill mannered as he speaks this. "Robinson," said Delamarche, "That's a fine way of talking. He's a German all right. You did warn me against him at the beginning, but I'm a kind-hearted fool and so I let him come with us all the same. We've given him our confidence, we've dragged him with us all day and lost half a day at least on his account, and now—just because he's chummed up with somebody at the hotel—he gives us the go-by, simply gives us the go-by. But because he's a lying German he doesn't do it frankly but makes his box a pretext, and being an ill-mannered German he can't leave us without insulting our honour and calling us thieves, just because we had a little fun with his box."

Karl, who is packing his things, says without turning round: "The more you say, the easier you make it for me to leave you. I know quite well what friendship is. I have had friends in Europe too and none of them can accuse me of ever behaving falsely or meanly to him. I'm not in touch with them now, naturally, but if I ever go back to Europe again they'll all be glad to see me, and they'll welcome me at once as a friend."

Then Karl thinks of a family photo which the two have either hidden or destroyed. It represents his painful alienation from the paternal sphere and prompts his corresponding desire to heal this wound.

Later Karl stays with at Hotel Occidental and he is well treated there. "Listen, wouldn't you like to take a job here in the hotel?" asked the Manageress.

"Very much," says Karl, "but I have terribly little experience. For instance, 1 can't even use a typewriter."

"That's not very important," says the Manageress.

"You're a German, aren't you?"

"Yes," said Karl, "I haven't been long in America."

"Where do you come from?"

"From Prague, in Bohemia," says Karl.

"Just think of that!" cries the Manageress in English with a strong German inflection, almost flinging her hands in the air. "Then we're compatriots, for my name is Grete Mitzelbach and I come from Vienna. And I know Prague quite well; I worked for half a year in the 'Golden Goose' in Wenceslaus Square. Only think of that!!"

But all at once, becoming animated again, she seizes both Karl's hands and cries: "Now that you turn out to be a countryman of mine, you mustn't go away on any account. You mustn't offend me by doing that. How would you like, for instance, to be a lift-boy? Just say the word and it's done. If you've seen something of this country, you'll realize that it isn't very easy to get such posts, for they're the best start in life that you can think of. You come in contact with all the hotel guests, people are always seeing you and giving you little errands to do; in short, every day you have the chance to better yourself. I'll fix everything up for you; leave it to me."

The Manageress provides Karl a room and a liftboy job. Later, Karl when he is to sleep, Therese Berchtold, Manageress's secretary meets him. She provides Karl an excellent company. Kafka develops a deep and affectionate attachment between the two.

Then Karl reports to the Head Waiter, under whose direction he is to be, a slender, handsome man with a big nose, who might well have been in the forties. The Head Waiter has no time to exchange even a word with him and simply rings for a lift-boy, who chances to be the very one that Karl saw the previous day. The Head Waiter calls him only by his first name, Giacomo, but it takes Karl some time to identify the name, for in the English pronunciation it is unrecognizable. The boy is instructed to show Karl all the duties of a lift-boy.

After the very week Karl realizes that he is quite equal to the job.

Karl is allowed to sleep in a dormitory. Kafka describes: "As a quiet place to sleep in the dormitory, certainly left much to be desired. For each boy had his own time-table for eating, sleeping, recreation and incidental services during his free twelve hours; so that the place was always in a turmoil."

Once a week, on changing from day to night duty, he has a free period of 24 hours, part of which he devots to seeing the Manageress once or twice and exchanging a few words with Therese.

During the month and a half that Karl stays at Rameses, he is only thrice in Therese's room for long visits of a few hours at a time. It is naturally smaller than the Manageress's rooms; the few things in it are crowded round the window; but after his experience in the dormitory Karl appreciates the value of a private, relatively quiet room, and though he never expressly says so. Therese can see how much he liked being there. She has no secrets from him, and indeed it would not have been very easy to keep secrets from him after that visit of hers on the first night. She is an illegitimate child; her father was a foreman mason who had sent for her and her mother from Pomerania; but as if that had been his whole duty, or as if the work-worn woman and the sickly child whom he met at the landing-stage had disappointed his expectations, he had gone off to Canada without much explanation shortly after their arrival, and they had received neither a letter nor any other word from him, which indeed was not wholly surprising, for they were lost beyond discovery among the tenements in the east end of New York.

Then Therese narrates the tragic death of her mother. Now the Manageress is helpful to her. Therese's story reminds us Hardy's Newman, his wife Susan and their daughter Elizabeth-Jane.

A hotel boy Rennel speaks to Karl of Delamarche's visit for Karl. Karl, however avoids both Delamarche and Robinson.

The next chapter (6) is "The Case of Robinson." One day Robinson, quite drunk, meets Karl.

"Wouldn't you like to come and see us, Rossmann? We're living in great style now," says Robinson, leering seductively at Karl.

"Does the invitation come from you or from Delamarche?" asks Karl.

"From me and Delamarche. Both of us together," says Robinson.

"Then let me tell you, and you can pass it on to Delamarche: that break between us, if it wasn't obvious enough to you at the time, was final. You two have done me more harm than anyone else has ever done. Can you have taken it into your heads not to leave me in peace even now?"

"But we're your friends," says Robinson disgustingly, maudlin tears rising to his eyes. "Delamarche asked me to tell you that he'll make it all upto you. We're living now with Brunelda, a lovely singer." And at the name he starts to sing in a high quavering voice, but Karl silences him in time, hissing at him: "Shut your mouth this minute; don't you know where you are?"

"Rossmann," said Robinson, intimidated as far as singing was concerned, "I'm a friend of yours, I am; say what you like. And now you've got such a fine job here, couldn't you lend me something?"

A few hours later Robinson feels sick, because of alcoholism. He does not go. Karl puts him in his dorm. Meanwhile, the head waiter Isbary notices Karl's absence and summons him. He says, "You were absent from duty without leave. Do you know what that means? It means dismissal. I'll listen to no excuses, you can keep your lying apologies to yourself; the fact that you were not there is quite enough for me. If I once pass that over and let you off, all my forty lift-boys will soon be taking to their heels during working hours, and I'll be left to carry my five thousand guests up the stairs on my own shoulder."

The Head Porter Feodor, who is there, reproaches Karl.

Karl understands now that he has really lost his post, for the Head Waiter has already told him so and here is the Head Porter repeating it as an accomplished fact, and in the case of a lift-boy there is probably no need for the hotel management to confirm a dismissal.

Later Isbary informs Karl's dismissal to the Manageress. Though the manageress is positive about Karl, Isbary is deliberately negative against the innocent boy.

Shortly after, Therese arrives to the spot. We understand that the Manageress asks the Head Waiter to calm the boy. The Portor calls the boy back with force

"Please, Karl, come nearer," she says. Karl obeys, or rather is dragged nearer by the Head Porter. "Let him go, can't you?" says the Manageress in exasperation. "He isn't a murderer!" The Head Porter actually lets him go, but before doing so crushes his arm in a final grip so violently that the boy bursts into tears.

"Karl," says the Manageress, folding her hands calmly in her lap and looking at Karl with her head bent—it is not in the least like an interrogation—"first of all I want to tell you that I still have complete confidence in you."

Then the Head Waiter speaks of Robinson's sleeping at Karl's dorm and his quarrel with other boys. He adds details (though false) about Karl's friendship with the people in the town, and his night activities. This hurts the Manageress. So she consoles the boy, by giving him a letter of introduction to a friend in the city asking him to employ Karl. Therese weeps at Karl's departure. The Head Porter's torture to Karl is very sadistic

Remembering these things, Karl tells himself that he has suffered enough as a lift-boy and yet it has all been in vain, for his job has not proved, as he has hoped, a step to something higher, but has rather pushed him further down, and even brought him very near prison. On top of this, he is still in the clutches of the Head Porter, who is no doubt considering ways and means of putting him to greater shame. And quite forgetting that the Head Porter is the last man to listen to reason, Karl exclaims, striking his brow several times with the hand that happens to be free: "Even if I actually did pass you without a greeting, how can a grown man be so vindictive about such an omission!"

Then Karl leaves the Hotel Occidental. He walks fast. He turns round and notices in a small, low doorway, which looks like the entrance to a vault, a couple of lift-boys whom he knows well, straining and tugging at a stretcher on which, as he now perceives, Robinson is actually lying, his head, face and arms swathed in manifold bandages. It is horrible to see him lift his arms to his eyes to wipe away his tears with the bandages, tears of pain or grief or perhaps even of joy at seeing Karl again.

"Rossmann," he cries reproachfully, "why have you kept me waiting so long? For a whole hour I've been struggling to keep myself from being carted away before you came. These fellows, and he gives one of the lift-boys a clout on the head, as if his bandages secures him from retaliation "are absolute devils. Ah, Rossmann, I've had to pay dearly for this visit to you."

"Why, what have they been doing to you?" says Karl, stepping over to the stretcher, which the lift-boys laughingly set down so as to have a rest.

And so Karl settles himself besides Robinson, who leans his head against him. The two lift-boys heartily shake hands with him through the window, taking leave of their one-time colleague, and the taxi makes a sharp turn into the thoroughfare.

Chapter 7 is aptly called "A Refuge." Karl goes off, no doubt. The taxi is parked at a place where Delamarche stays. A policeman enquires of Karl. Unfortunately he harasses Karl and Karl runs off. Though two policemen try to catch him, they cannot. But Delamarche catches and consoles Karl. He takes him to his house where he lives with Brunelda, a separatee singer. Robinson serves Delamarche and Brunelda.

All the three rest for a while. Then Delamarche enquires for a woman called Brunelda. She is in a room where enter Delamarache and Karl. Karl looks at her and she feels awkward. She yet allows him stay. He says in gratitude: "I thank you anyway, for letting me stay here a little longer. I've had no sleep for twenty-four hours and I've done a lot of things and been rather upset. I'm terribly tired. I hardly know where I am. But after I have slept an hour or two you can pack me off straight away and I'll go gladly."

"You can stay here as long as you like," says the woman, adding ironically: "We have more than room enough here, as you see."

Kafka's description of Robinson and of Brunelda is a comic scene and the presentation is wonderful. Robinson speaks, "It's great fun for Brunelda. She only has to get an idea in her head that she's too cold, that she's too hot, that she wants to sleep, that she wants to comb her hair, that she wants to loosen her corset, that she wants to put it on, and then she has me sent on the balcony."

Robinson narrates his past after Karl left the two.

"For Brunelda had divorced her husband, was very wealthy and completely independent! She has sold everything she had for the sake of Delamarche, and has moved with all she possesses into this suburban flat in order to devote herself entirely to him with nobody to disturb her; besides, that is what Delamarche wanted too." So they dismissed all servants.

"So you've turned into Delamarche's servant, have you?" says Karl, summing up.

Then Robinson speaks elaborately as to how Karl can become Brunelda's servant.

But Karl does not like all this. He decides to find out a job in the great city.

Then there is a procession in the street. Karl hurries to get away. Soon the inside couple come out. Brunelda asks "Where are you going, boy?" Delamarche's severe eye holds Karl an instant and Brunelda draws him to her. "Don't you want to see the procession down there?" she says, pushing him before her to the railing.

The street demonstration is about a judge's election. Then Karl wants to get away. But Delamarche with a fight wants to retain him. He wants Karl to work as a servant. He locks the door. Karl escapes in the night. He meets Joseph Mendel, a salesman daytime, but a student at night time. But the student advises Karl to stay with Darlmarche better. Karl realizes that the student cannot advise him for a job where he serves; nor can he rescue him from the police; while Darlmarche could do both.

Still Karl leaves.

The novel breaks off after the seventh chapter, and starts afresh in the last, so far as one can see, simply because Kafka did not in all honesty see how the transition was to be made. He had met Felice since he began the novel, and the new spirit she engendered possibly introduced the figure of Fanny, together with the image of the theatre as a place which accepted as freely as a woman's love did. But Kafka was deeply sceptical; he saw no way of moving from Karl's position at the end of chapter and the ending. A gap was inevitable.

Chapter 8 is entitled "The Nature Theatre of Oklahoma."

At a street corner Karl notices a placard with the announcement: "The Oklahoma Theatre will engage members for its company today at Clayton race-course from six o'clock in the morning until midnight. The great Theatre of Oklahoma calls you!"

Karl takes a train to Clayton, a suburb in New York and notices a lot of theatrical din—his acquaintance Fanny is seen as a trumpeter for attracting job seekers. He asks her whether he can get a job there. She replies, "Most certainly why, it's the greatest theatre in the world. What a piece of luck that we're to be together again. All the same it depends on what job you get. For it would be quite possible for us not to see each other at all, even though we were both engaged here."

"Is the place really so big as that?" asks Karl.

"It's the biggest theatre in the world," Fanny says again. "I haven't seen it yet myself, I admit, but some of the other girls here, who have been in Oklahoma already, say that there are almost no limits to it."

Then Karl meets an official and speaks for a job. However, it seems that the competition for jobs has become lively. Karl feels very glad that he is such an early arrival, perhaps the first of them all; the married couple are apprehensive and ask various questions as to whether great demands would be made on them.

"But it's a theatre," thinks Karl dubiously, and he listens very intently.

"We have accordingly," goes on the staff manager, "set up employment bureaus in the bookmakers' booths, an office for each trade or profession."

One of them, who is obviously only a clerk, says: "Please give me your identity papers."

Karl, in fact, does not have his visa paper. Still he wants an engineer's job which he cannot get. Then Karl is taken to the employment office for European migrants, where he is employed.

Yet Karl calls himself a 'negro' here. This is quite awkward.

Helen Weinberg observes, "Why the name of 'Negro,' however, which he says is his nickname? Perhaps he is not as skeptical of the theater as one might assume from the evidence of a false name. Perhaps he is throwing off the past entirely, assuming a new identity for the new community and choosing his future in a new world. With his sixth sense of prophecy, Kafka seems to have realized that the Negro, enslaved and exploited, would become ultimately the fullest embodiment of a new, hopefully free, characteristically non-European man in America. Though victimized by the worldly people he meets, there is always the hope, the dream, of identity and freedom in the Nature Theater of Oklahoma. The recurring 'rebirths' implicit throughout the novel—leaving Europe; being rescued from the ship by Uncle Jacob: finding the Nature Theater—symbolize this ephemeral, ever present hope before the fully developed denouement of the Nature Theater chapter itself."

Karl is made a technical worker. But wherever he is to be taken now, he decides that he must first report to Fanny how well everything has gone. To his great sorrow he learns from the attendant that both the angels and the devils have already left for the next town on the recruiting squad's itinerary.

Karl then has a fine dinner there. He notices Giacomo of the Hotel Occidental there. Because after dismissal he joins the theatre company. He remembers the Manageress and Therese.

"I hope," says the staff manager, "that you have been satisfied with our reception of you and the dinner we have given you. The recruiting squad is generally supposed to keep a good kitchen. I'm sorry we must clear the table already, but the train for Oklahoma is going to leave in five minutes."

When they reach the station the train is ready for departure. People in the station point out the newcomers to each other, and one hears an exclamation such as: "All these belong to the Theatre of Oklahoma!" The theatre seems to be much better known than Karl has assumed; of course, he has never taken much interest in theatrical affairs.

Karl gets a window seat, with Giacomo beside him. So they sit, the two of them, close together, rejoicing in their hearts over the journey.

For two days and two nights they journey on. Only now does Karl understand how huge America is.

Ronald Gray thinks Kafka based his novel on Charles Dickens' *David Copperfield* which Kafka read. Some years later, Kafka observed, while reading *David Copperfield*, that "The Stoker," and even more the novel he had intended to follow it, was "sheer imitation of Dickens." He mentions several incidents common to the two novels, whose heroes are clearly similar as young boys cast adrift in a heartless world. One sees, too, that the encounter with the stoker has something in common with Pip's encounter with Magwitch at the start of *Great Expectations*. Kafka's admiration of Dickens's "opulence and carefree, powerful prodigality," is, however, tinged with criticism, to the effect that this leads to a meaningless or senseless whole, a fault which he believes himself to have avoided. Yet despite Kafka's modesty here, one cannot feel that he has judged these two novels well.

As his own progresses, Karl meets a variety of people, most of them exploiting him, just as David does. But it is a journey into nowhere, with no end in view. Where David moves from Yarmouth or Dover or Canterbury to London and back, as to a centre, Karl simply moves on. David has good angels to counter the evil ones, a Betsy Trotwood for a Murdstone, a Peggotty for a Uriah Heep; Karl has only the Manageress at the Ramses Hotel to speak for him, and she gives him up in a crisis. Dickens moves up character after character to keep the reader of his serial agog, which results in the richness Kafka speaks of, and does have a disorienting effect; Dickens does, however, weave them into a far-flung plot, which they reappear to promote. According to Gray, Kafka's novel is much different from Dickens. He observes, "Kafka's new characters are not only fewer and less idiosyncratic and less memorable than Micawber and Creakle, they appear only to be forgotten again. One looks in vain for any guiding thought in *America*, any balance of forces or intentional shaping, anything to match, say, the reflections on love and marriage aroused by David and Steerforth; there is simply the not highly inventive sequence of seedy figures."

As for Karl's life in America, Karl suffers unduly. His dismissal from the job as a lift-boy in the Hotel Occidental would have been relished by every reader of Victorian sentimental fiction: having repeatedly and unselfishly stood in for another lift-boy in exacting conditions of work, he chances to leave his own post for two minutes on an errand of mercy, is discovered by the head-porter, abandoned by the cook, who is overwhelmed by the spurious proofs of his depravity, discharged with ignominy, and denounced in front of a policeman by the very friend on whose account he had momentarily left the lift unattended. The policeman then refuses to believe a word Karl says, but is overwhelmed when one of the hoboes shows evidence of genteel respectability by producing a visiting-card. Such incidents continue to the penultimate chapter, and seem designed to confirm the sense Karl already has, that the world is thronged with personal enemies of his. The perennial 'I am Innocent' was never more piercingly implied.

Kafka's hero Karl is just 15 years old. Still he is sent to America because he impregnated a maid and she got a child. This is under duress. As critics think Karl's parents' stand is not justified in the novel. After reading the novel, we hardly believe that Karl is much interested in sex. It is observed, "Certainly Karl has had no joy of his first sexual experience with a woman, and his second ends in a jiu-jitsu fight. The stoker and one of the lift boys may represent a homosexual attraction for him, but this is also a point which Kafka does not explore. Karl has more sympathy from the woman cook and Therese than any he knew before, and in the final chapter he meets Fanny, whom he has evidently got to know affectionately at some point in the unwritten pages. But if this is development it is thinly sketched in, and nothing comes of it, since after meeting Fanny Karl leaves her again, almost at once, and is last seen in the company of another lift-boy, Giacomo. Love for either sex is never actually touched on, and if Kafka meant a development to be seen he left very few pointers."

What is the point of Karl's repeated association with a pair of men, first Pollunder and Green, then Robinson and Delamarche? Such pairs are seen in Shakespeare's *Hamlet*, and Samuel Beckett's *Waiting for Godot,* for example. There seems to be an affinity here with the pairs in other novels of Kafka's: Franz and Willem in *The Trial*, Arthur and Jeremias in *The Castle*.

The final chapter is a different matter, in almost every respect. Strictly speaking the chapter as printed is not a final chapter, but, as the MS shows, joins a penultimate chapter with the beginning of what may be taken as the really final chapter, which breaks off. Nor did Kafka supply for it the title "The Oklahoma Nature-Theatre," which was supplied by Max Brod: the MS gives no title for the chapter, which is presumably the one written, according to the diary, late in 1914 and 'Nature Theatre' is an expression not found in the text. Still, it is clear that an entirely fresh start has been made, which may end happily with Karl's acceptance by the theatre, or may merely lead to his total disappearance from human society. In fact, the original title for the novel was *The Man Who Disappeared.*

Up to this point, Karl has met almost nothing but hostility and injustice. The invitation to join the Theatre of Oklahoma suddenly provides a world where nothing is hostile and there is no injustice. The Oklahoma Theatre accepts everybody, no matter what his qualification or background. It is not even interested in the veracity of the answers given to its employment agency, with the result that Karl is admitted under the surname 'Negro,' as a technical assistant. The other America of his earlier experience is a long way off.

Ronald Gray, a well-known Kafka scholar, observes, "All this might suggest that Karl had somehow won through, rather in accordance with what Max Brod believed the intended ending to have been. If one wanted to interpret in a religious sense—though the only justification for this is in the crude alternation of angels and devils outside the recruiting booth, and the curse uttered in the advertisement—one might say Karl had come to salvation or that his acceptance by the theatre is a kind of religious conversion, which is what one interpreter says. 'Everything he had done up to now was forgotten, nobody was going to reproach him with it anymore,' Kafka writes, and though Karl has not done anything very reproachable in the novel as it stands, his relief is understandable. It is still not a matter of forgiveness or sympathetic comprehension. Karl is still as eager to please as ever, he submits to authority with the same gratification, and though he has some brief doubts about how a theatre can guarantee to find jobs for all professions, the doubts do not last long."

There is also in *America* a 'Castle', if one takes the castle as a goal which the hero is determined to reach. There is the continent into which Karl penetrates further and further, without knowing where he is going or what he is looking for, and there is the Theatre of Oklahoma, suddenly emerging as though it were what Karl had been seeking all along.

Identity crisis is one of the themes of the novel *America*. The passport found in the suitcase is the official document which endorses the immigrant's identity. It attests to his name as well as to his place and date of birth. It should also contain the visa which gives the immigrant official entry rights and entitles him to work and to settle down.

"The Metamorphosis" and "The Judgement," are the two stories which Kafka considered combining with "The Stoker" under the title *The Sons*. In all three stories the metropolis of New York is characterized as a space which defamiliarises all kinship relations.

Max Brod says, "Kafka knew quite well, and discussed the fact, that this novel was more optimistic and 'lighter' in mood than any of his other 'writings.'" The novel is ambivalent: both pessimism and optimism are present in it.

America has its own completeness in spite of its rambling episodic form; and it has its own complexity of intertwined, contradictory themes in spite of its seeming simplicity.

Helen Weinburg observes, "If Franz Kafka was the most private of modern writers, driven by some deeply personal impulse to polish his language and his stories so that they might dazzle with truth, he has also become the twentieth-century writer whose impact on modem literary consciousness is most vividly felt. More than Proust, Joyce, or Mann, he appears to anticipate in his work a post-religious spiritual awareness that is ever more present in literature as the century ages. His influence, if it may be called that, is indirect and not of the manner proposed by historians of national literary periods. As a regionalist of the spirit, Kafka evades categorizing in any of the textbook ways. He had a primary, pure, and intuitive some say neurotic-grasp of those themes that belong to all of us in the modern world, and by articulating them he has also in a way given them to us."

The Trial

> Then suddenly the scene
> Changed, and the unbroken dream entangled me
> In long orations, which I strove to plead
> Before unjust tribunals—with a voice
> Labouring, a brain confounded, and a sense,
> Death-like, of treacherous desertion, felt
> In the last place of refuge—my own soul.
>
> —*William Wordsworth*

Franz Kafka has influenced the modern times. He is known as the poster-boy of modern age's sense of alienation as Anthony Burgess records in his book *The Novels Now* (1967). Kafka's place in modern Europe is special. His three novels *The Trial* (1925), *America* (1927) and *The Castle* (1926) and short stories have affected literary discourses not only in Europe but also in the rest of the world.

The present English translation of *The Trial* by Breon Mitchell, a Professor of Germanic studies and comparative literature at Indiana University, America, is based on the restored text. The translation is an accomplishment of the highest order that will honor Kafka far into the twenty-first century as Walter Abish feels. Mitchell sets a new standard: "Careful precision regarding Kafka's 'legalese' is alchemically fused with a prose of great verve and intense readability." What critics argue is that Kafka did not rewrite or edit his works; and apparently, the chapterization is haphazard. There remain certain inconsistencies. Kafka constantly distorts time and space and often underlines the frailty of human perception.

The translator says, "*The Trial* begins as a farce and ends in tragedy. The opening chapter has a strong theatrical air, complete with an audience across the way. Later that evening, when Josef K. reenacts the scene for an amused Fraulein Burstner, who has just returned from the theater herself, he takes on both his own role and that of his accuser, replaying the farce, shouting his own name aloud with comedic consequences. The final chapter of the novel offers a carefully balanced counterpart in which the men who are sent for him, like pair of old supporting actors. Stage the final scene in the deserted quarry before yet another audience at a distant window. But this time no one is laughing."

Breon Mitchell feels the dominant discourse in *The Trial* is of course legal. Some feel that the whole of the novel is written in legalese. Mitchell tells, "Over the course of a year, Josef K. gradually weakens in his struggle with the mysterious forces that surround him. His true trial begins with the first sentence and ends only with his death."

The Trial has a complex presentation. A look at the contents reveals this amply. The first chapter "Arrest" begins with a shock: "Someone must have slandered Josef K., for one morning, without having done anything wrong, he was arrested." Josef K., the hero of the novel is arrested in his rented lodge. Many others including his friend Fraulein Burstner stay in the same lodge. Kafka describes K. as "slender yet solidly built, and was wearing a fitted black jacket, which, like a traveler's outfit, was provided with a variety of pleats, pockets, blankets, buttons and a belt, and thus appeared eminently practical, although its purpose remained obscure". The two guards, Franz and Wilhem, and their inspector have led to his arrest. K. wanted breakfast from his servant Anna of Frau Grubach.

Why Josef K. was arrested is a mystery. The authorial comment appears to be this: "After all Josef K., 'K.' for short, lived in a state governed by law, there was universal peace, all statutes were in force; who dared assault him in his own lodgings? He'd always tended to take things lightly, to believe the worst only when it arrived, making no provision for the future, even when things looked bad." Josef K. is 30 and the day of his arrest is his birth day. This is an irony.

On being arrested K. thinks of committing suicide. Then he thinks why he should do so. This is rather autobiographical. Shortly the inspector meets and expresses his surprise to have arrested K. who enquires: "Who's accusing me? What authorities are in charge of the proceedings? Are you officials? No one's wearing a uniform, unless you want to call your suit" – he turned to Franz – "a uniform, but it's more like a traveler's outfit. I demanded clarification on these matters, and I'm convinced that once they've been clarified we can part on the friendliest of terms." He feels "The arrest is completely senseless." The inspector allows K. to do his work at the bank. K. is a prominent officer in the bank. But the inspector places three of K.'s colleagues – Rabensteiner, Kullich and Kaminer – to guard K.'s activities.

The next chapter "Conversation with Frau Grubach." Fraulein Burstner narrates the story further. It is said the morning event put Frau Grubach's activities in disarray. K. meets Frau Brubach and speaks to her of his arrest. The lady, however, simply says that the arrest is scholarly. K. wants to know the whereabouts of Fraulein Burstner, for he wants to tender her his apology as his arrester the Inspector and his two guards used and defiled her room in the morning. Now the young lady has gone to film. He waits for her. She comes at 11.30 midnight. Still K. meets her eagerly. Both discuss the matter. The lady checks her room of any disturbance. The lady is to serve as a secretary in a law firm and K. asks her to help him with information later. The two love each other. Now they are a bit scarred of chit-chat as Frau Grubach's nephew Lanz is taking rest in the next room. So K. returns to his room.

"Initial Inquiry" is the next chapter. K. is informed by telephone that a small inquiry into his affair would take place the following Sunday. Sunday is chosen because that day is a holiday. So K. rushes to the said place Juliusstrasse for the inquiry. That place is in a distant area in the same city. The weather is dull and K. is tired. Kafka describes elaborately the locale and the prevailing confusion about the address.

K. reaches the court. He knows he is late and he confesses: "I may have arrived late, but I'm here now."

K. tells the examining magistrate: "Listen: around ten days ago I was arrested; the arrest itself makes me laugh, but that's another matter. I was assaulted in the morning in bed; perhaps they'd been ordered to arrest some house painter–that can't be ruled out after what the examining magistrate has said–someone as innocent as I am, but they chose me. The room next door had been taken over by two coarse guards, Willem and Franz. If I had been a dangerous thief, they couldn't have taken better precautions. These guards were corrupt ruffians as well; they talked my ear off, they wanted bribes, they tried to talk to me out of my undergarments and clothes under false pretenses, they wanted money, supposedly to bring me breakfast, after they'd shamelessly eaten my own breakfast before my very eyes. And that wasn't all. I was led into a third room to see the inspector. It was the room of a young woman for whom I have the highest respect, yet I was forced to look on while this room was defiled, so to speak, by the presence of the guards and the inspector, on my account, but through no fault of my own. It wasn't easy to stay calm. However, I managed to, and I asked the inspector quite calmly–if he were here he'd have to confirm that–why I had been arrested. And what was the reply of this inspector, whom I still see before me, sitting on the chair of the young woman I mentioned, the very image of mindless arrogance? Gentlemen, he really had no reply at all, perhaps he actually knew nothing, he had arrested me and that was enough for him. He had taken the additional step of bringing to the young lady's room three minor employees from my bank, which spent their time fingering photographs, the property of the lady, and mixing them all up. The presence of these served another purpose, of course: they were meant, like my landlady and her maid, to spread the news of my arrest, damage my public reputation, and in particular to undermine my position at the bank. Well, none of this met with the slightest success; even my landlady, very simple person–I pronounce her name in all honor, she's called Frau Grubach–even Frau Grubach was sensible enough to release that an arrest like that means as little as a mugging on the street by teenage hoodlums. I repeat, the whole affair has merely caused me some unpleasantness and temporary annoyance, but might it not have had more serious consequences as well." K. blames of an evil organization behind his arrest. In his view, "That organization engages corrupt guards, inane inspectors and examining magistrates who are at best mediocre, but that supports as well a system of judges of all ranks." The magistrate pronounces, "That you have today deprived yourself–although you can't yet have realized it–of the advantage that an interrogation offers to the arrested man in each case." K. laughs at the door. "You scoundrels," he cries, "you can have all your interrogation." K. stands eye to eye facing the crowd.

The next chapter is "In the Empty Courtroom: the Student, the Officials." K. goes to the same building the next Sunday. A watcher woman says there is no session today. K. looks at law books kept over there. He looks at a book entitled: *The Torments Grete Suffered at the Hands of Her Husband Hans.* He finds that her husband is a servant in the court. K. thinks of making use of his service. He finds a servant there by the name Bertold. The latter is referred to as 'student' and he happens to be the information officer. The lady (Elsa) loves K. She seems to be a prostitute. She has an affair with the watchman referred to as student. Next situation is with the lady's husband. When her husband comes to see her she has gone with the 'man student.' He says, "They are always taking her from me." There is a reference to her having an affair with the court officials including the magistrate. The author says K. loses the information officer's favour by his rude behaviour.

In the next chapter "The Flogger" we see certain bad happenings. As K. accused to the magistrate during his first trial that his guards ate his breakfast and behaved uncivilly, the two guards are punished with flogging one day. The inspector punishes them though K. asks him to be soft at that. K. says, "I don't even consider them guilty; it's the organization that's guilty, it's the high officials who are guilty."

"The Uncle – Leni" is the next chapter. K. has an uncle called Albert. The Uncle has brought him up. Today he has come to enquire K. about his arrest. He is much upset. His first question on arrival is: "What's this I hear, Josef?". Albert accuses K. of his bad attitude and he is afraid that K. is ruining the family honour. Both go to see the familiar lawyer Huld. They find that Huld is ill. Leni, the servant of the house does not like to entertain them. Still Albert has his own way and he meets Huld forcibly.

The two outsiders discuss the matter of arrest and the way to come out of the enquiry. Huld examines K.'s case carefully though he is ill. He requests the court clerk for K.'s rescue. Whereas K. chats with Leni, the nurse who it appears is the lawyer's mistress. Once the two come outside the Uncle says K.: "We're trying to figure out the best way to help you, I have to handle the lawyer carefully, he has to handle the chief clerk the same way, and you have every reason to at least offer me support."

The next chapter is "Lawyer, Manufacturer, Painter." The thought of trial never leaves Josef K. Now and anon he thinks of submitting a written defense to the court. The court proceedings are very bad, for there is no scope for an accused to employ a lawyer. The system is unorganized and inhuman. The author says, "If he had been alone in the world he could have easily disregarded the trial, although then the trial would surely never have occurred at all. But now his uncle had already taken him to the lawyer, and family considerations were involved; his job was no longer totally independent of the course of the trial, he himself had been incautious enough to mention the trial to a few acquaintances with a certain inexplicable feeling of self-satisfaction, others had heard about it in unknown ways, his relationship to Fraulein Burstner seemed to fluctuate with the trial itself–in short, it was no longer a matter of accepting or rejecting the trial, he was in the middle of it and had to defend himself. If he was tired, he was in trouble."

When K. is in the bank he finds two business people. One of the two – the manufacturer – suggests him to see his painter

Titorelli. He says everyone has a problem: "Each of us has his cross to bear" (p. 134). K. meets the painter and the latter welcomes him as though he has gone there for a painting. K. hears that Titorelli is a court painter as his father had been once. The painting was for witness in the days when photography was not in vogue. Then Titorelli speaks of three kinds of acquittals–actual acquittal, apparent acquittal and protraction. The first kind of acquittal is good but difficult. Finally K. buys some paintings particularly "A Landscape of the Heath."

The next week K. decides to dismiss the lawyer Huld. He meets him. Before that he discusses the matter with Huld's ancther client Block, the merchant. The latter tells him that he has been on trial for the last five years. Yet he has four more lawyer plus shysters apart from Huld. The short of it is that the court proceedings are complex. Still both Block and the lady Leni advise K. not to dismiss the lawyer. K., as a clean and straight man, tells the lawyer: "I wanted to tell you that as of today I no longer wish for you to represent me." Huld is annoyed. He says he supported his case just because he was his friend Albert's nephew.

The chapter "In the Cathedral" depicts the final part of the tragedy. K. has an Italian business associate and the latter wants to see the architecture of a cathedral. The Manager asks K. to show the same to him, for K. knows Italian. So K. goes to a certain cathedral and waits for the guest. Unfortunately the guest does not come and it also rains. Finally K. enters a cathedral where he was waiting and meets the chaplain who happens to be the court chaplain. The chaplain knows K.'s case very well. K. notices a young woman before the statue of Madonna.

"You are Joseph K.?" says the priest, lifting one hand from the balustrade in a vague gesture. "Yes," says K., thinking how frankly he used to give his name and what a burden it had recently become to him; nowadays people he had never seen before seem to know his name. How pleasant it was to have to introduce oneself before being recognized! "You are an accused man," says the priest in a very low voice: "Yes," says K., "so I have been informed."

"Then you are the man I seek," says the priest. "I am the prison chaplain."

"Indeed," says K.

"I had you summoned here," says the priest, "to have a talk with you."

"I didn't know that," says K. "I came here to show an Italian round the Cathedral."

"A mere detail," says the priest. "What is that in your hand? Is it a prayer-book?"

"No," replies K., "it is an album of sights worth seeing in the town."

"Lay it down," says the priest.

K. pitches it away so violently that it flies open and slides some way along the floor with dishevelled leaves.

"Do you know that your case is going badly?" asks the priest.

"I have that idea myself," says K. "I've done what I could, but without any success so far. Of course, my first petition hasn't been presented yet.'"

"How do you think it will end?" asks the priest.

"At first I thought it must turn out well," says K., "but now I frequently have my doubts. I don't know how it will end. Do you?"

"No," says the priest, "but I fear it will end badly. You are held to be guilty. Your case will perhaps never get beyond a lower Court. Your guilt is supposed, for the present, at least, to have been proved."

"But I am not guilty," says K., "it's a misunderstanding. And if it comes to that, how can any man be called guilty? We are all simply men here, one as much as the other."

"That is true," says the priest, "but that's how all guilty men talk."

"Are you prejudiced against me too?" asks K.

"I have no prejudices against you," says the priest.

"I thank you," says K., "but all the others who are concerned in these proceedings are prejudiced against me. They are influencing even outsiders. My position is becoming more and more difficult."

"You are misinterpreting the facts of the case," says the priest. "The verdict is not so suddenly arrived at, the proceedings only gradually merge into the verdict."

"So that's how it is," says K., letting his head sink.

"What is the next step you propose to take in the matter?" asks the priest.

"I'm going to get more help," says K., looking up again to see how the priest took his statement. "There are several possibilities I haven't explored yet."

"You cast about too much for outside help," says the priest disapprovingly, "especially from women. Don't you see that it isn't the right kind of help?"

"In some cases, even in many I could agree with you," says K., "but not always."

The church man with a metaphor of guard anticipates K.'s doom.

In the final chapter "The End" we see that K. is escorted by two strangers. "So they came quickly out of the town, which at this point merged almost without transition into the open fields. A small stone quarry, deserted and bleak, lay quite near to a still completely urban house. Here the two men came to a standstill, whether because this place had been their goal from the very beginning or because they were too exhausted to go farther. Now they loosened their hold of K., who stood waiting dumbly, took off the top-hats and wiped the sweat from their brows with pocket handkerchiefs, meanwhile surveying the quarry. The moon shone down on everything with that simplicity and serenity which no other light possesses."

After an exchange of courteous formalities regarding which of them is to take preference in the next task—these emissaries seem to have been given no specific assignments in the charge laid jointly upon them—one of them comes K. and removes his coat, his waistcoat, and finally his shirt. K. shivers involuntarily, whereupon the man gives him a light, reassuring pat on the back. Then he folds the clothes carefully together, as if they are likely to be used again at some time, although perhaps not immediately. Not to leave K. standing motionless, exposed to the night breeze, which is chilly enough, he takes him by the arm and walks him up and down a little, while his partner investigates the quarry to find a suitable spot. When he find it he beckons, and K.'s companion leads him over there. It is a spot near the cliff-side where a loose boulder is lying. The two of them lay K. down on the ground, prop him against the boulder, and settle his head upon it. But in spite of the pains they take and all the willingness K. shows, his posture remains contorted and unnatural-looking. So one of the men begs the other to let him dispose K. all by himself, yet even that does not improve matters. Finally they leave K. in a position which is not even the best of the positions they have already rehearsed. Then one of them opens his frock-coat and out of a sheath that hangs from a belt girt round his waistcoat draws a long, thin, double-edged butcher's knife, holds it up, and testes the cutting edges in the moonlight. Once more the odious ceremonial of courtesy begins, the first hands the knife across K. to the second, who hands it across K. back again to the first. K. now perceives clearly that he is supposed to seize the knife himself, as it travels from hand to hand above him, and plunges it into his own breast. But he does not do so, he merely turns his head, which is still free to move, and gazes around him. He cannot completely rise to the occasion, he cannot relieve the officials of all their tasks; the responsibility for this last failure of his lies with him who has not left him the remnant of strength necessary for the deed. His glance falls on the top storey of the house adjoining the quarry. With a flicker as of a light going up, the casements of a window there suddenly flies open; a human figure, faint and insubstantial at that distance and that height, leans abruptly far forward and stretches both arms still farther. Who is it? A friend? A good man? Someone who sympathizes? Someone who wants to help? Is it one person only? Or are they all there? Is help at hand? Are there some arguments in his favour that have been overlooked? Of course there must be. Logic is doubtless unshakeable, but it cannot withstand a man who wants to go on living. Where is the Judge whom he has never seen? Where is the High Court, to which he has never penetrated? He raises his hands and spreads out all his fingers.

But the hands of one of the partners are already at K.'s throat, while the other thrusts the knife into his heart and turns it there twice. With failing eyes K. can still see the two of them, cheek leaning against cheek, immediately before his face, watching the final act. "Like a dog!" he says: it is as if he meant the shame of it to outlive him. The two strangers stab him to death "Like a dog." K. is killed on his thirty-first birthday which he wanted to celebrate with his mother.

Albert Camus who, in a way, happened to succeed Franz Kafta, in his depiction of the absurd in life, observes, "In *The Trial,* Josef K. is accused. But he doesn't know of what. He is doubtless eager to defend himself, but he doesn't know why." Andre Gide writes, "The anguish that pervades this book is at some moments almost intolerable, for how should one not say, this hounded creature is myself? Anyone who has submitted to the experience of the novel knows that to be true. Within those confines one is stifled along with Joseph K., baffled by the same endless arguments, confused by the inscrutability of the Court, and relieved when execution is carried out and the claustrophobia ends. It seems to be not merely Joseph K.'s world, either. *The Trial* takes place for the most part in a perfectly ordinary setting, in a modem *pension*, in a bank, in tenement buildings, in offices where there are files and safes; only occasionally does it move to stranger places, the cathedral in complete darkness, the attic with its court officials, the magistrates' court off a remote staircase. So the suggestion often is that this is a commonly accepted world, the world as conventionally seen, but seen through to its depths. There is a Court under every roof, and K.'s uncle as well as his landlady, Frau Grubach, are aware of it although they rarely talk about it. The effect is more telling than a more romantic setting would have been, in pressing upon the reader Kafka's own experience of dread." Not only Kafka's. Martin Greenberg quotes with surprising appositeness lines from William Wordsworth as cited as the epitaph for the article.

The point about the trial in the novel is that there is no specific accusation. When K. asks, at his arrest, what he is charged with, he is told that while there is no possibility of error, the Court is 'attracted' by guilt, which can thus, evidently, not be in doubt. But there is never any definition even of the kind of guilt that might be in question. Perhaps, as Martin Greenberg says, "Joseph K.'s wrongdoing consists in the com plaint, which he never ceases making until just before the end, that a wrong has been done to him." But if the readers are able to see that, when K. cannot, we are placed in an embarrassingly superior position. To know the answer to K.'s problems in such a way is to remove oneself from the experience of the novel. Similarly, the explanation sometimes offered that K. is at fault because he visits a woman once a week "for hygienic reasons," is conventional in its disapprobation such visits may have been valuable to K. for the reason given, and that is literally all we know about them. To suggest that the whole mechanism of the Court was brought into play for so minor a sin is almost as absurd as the fact which is insisted on all through the book, that K. is never charged with anything.

'Yet another explanation that has been put forward is of a political kind. It is noticeable, for instance, that the First Interrogation takes place in a poor quarter of the town, quite unlike K.'s own quarter, and since the assembly of people there is compared with a 'political meeting,' it has been suggested that K. is on trial for his political beliefs or perhaps for his lack of political activity. (Max Brod's list of variant readings states that Kafka had originally written 'Socialist meeting.' This interpretation was given some additional weight by Klaus Wagenpach's revelation that Kafka had been interested in anarchist movements of his time, and had attended meetings of the 'Klub mladijch,' which was under police supervision. Wilhelm Emrich thinks that K. is a typical bourgeois on trial for antisocial behavior.

Fatemeh Mohammatadi observes, "The purpose of this is to examine man's alienation in contact with the other. In this situation, man finds himself alone without any protection. Man himself is hunted with compelling position. Kafka pictures man as a defenseless creator. He cannot defend himself because he is only a void being. He lets the other come in his being. This exposure of his being leads him to annihilation. Josef K. in this regard is a good sample for this purpose. He lets the court as a symbol of the other run his daily life and even he accepts the punishment which has been imposed upon him. This is the darkest form of alienation which happens to him."

Frank Magil observes, "It is observed that *The Trial* is one of the most effective and most discussed works to come out of Central Europe between wars. To many, perhaps most, readers it is a highly engaging comedy filled with buffoonery and fantasy. More serious students of literature see in it, however, a vast symbolism and a first rate psychological study of a system whose leaders are convinced of their own righteousness. To some the court is a symbol of the Church as an imperfect bridge between the individual and God. To others the symbolism represents rather the search of a sensitive Jew of a homeland that is always denied him. At any rate *The Trial* is a powerful and provocative book."

The Castle

Franz Kafka's novel *The Castle* is a mixture of both *The Trial* as an absurd story and *America* as a fantasy. It begins in a dreamy atmosphere. It is late one day evening and K. arrives there. The village is deep in snow. He visits the Bridg Inn, and rests.

No sooner he rests than he is rudely awakened by the castellan Schwazer. The later asks K. for permission to stay in the Castle village which belongs to the Count West-west. The prevailing atmosphere is much feudal. K. bursts forth sharply: "Enough of this fooling. You're going a little too far, my good fellow, and I'll have something to say tomorrow about your conduct. The landlord here and those other gentlemen will bear me out if necessary. Let me tell you that I am the Land Surveyor whom the Count is expecting. My assistants are coming tomorrow in a carriage with the apparatus. I did not want to miss the chance of a walk through the snow, but unfortunately lost my way several times and so arrived very late. That it was too late to present myself at the Castle. I knew very well before you saw fit to inform me. That is why I have made shift with this bed for the night, where, to put it mildly, you have had the discourtesy to disturb me. That is all I have to say. Good night, gentlemen." K. turned over on his side towards the stove."

Schwazer telephones to the authority and finds that what K. tells is true. K. sleeps soundly.

K. the nest day, finds the village not clear in snow. It is a hill village, and the so called Castle is on the hill yonder. There are peoples' house all around.

The Castle looks a wretched town at close quarers. K. compares the Castle to his native town, and feels that the castle is inferior. He meets a teacher and his batch of children. The teacher, after 'good morning,' asks whether K. does not like the Castle, as later K. asks the teacher whether he does not like the Count. Both part friendly. K. feels tired to visit the actual Castle afar.

K. then visits a peasant called Hans Brunswick. He notices a lot of hustle-bustle there. Then he rises to go. A man called Gerstacker drops him to the inn by his sledge.

Chapter 2 begins with a description about K.'s assistants and K.'s work as a land surveyor. In the previous chapter we learn that K.'s two assistants would report to him for duty. But Arthur and Jeremiah, the two assistants who report to him for duty are strangers. K. admits he is also a stranger in the village. Yet the assistants are known to be not strangers in the village, and by all means, they are employed in the Castle secretly.

K. asks them to maintain confidentiality and to work together. He calls both as Aurther, showing his infirmness in mind. He asks Arthur to get a sledge so that he can visit the Castle, but the two confide to him that none can visit the Castle without a permit. K. wants to apply for a permit. Soon the Castle servant Barnabus, as the messenger, delivers K. the letter which reads thus : "My dear Sir, as you know, you have been engaged for the Count's service. Your immediate superior is the Superintendent of the village, who will give you all particulars about your work and the terms of your employment, and to whom you are responsible. I myself, however, will try not to lose sight of you. Barnabas, the bearer of this letter, will report himself to you from time to time to learn your wishes and communicate them to me. You will find me always ready to oblige you, in so far as that is possible. I desire my workers to be contented". The signature is illegible, but stamped beside it is 'Chief of Department X.'

K. befriends the messenger Barnabus as he is much reticent with the peasants at the inn. He walks with the messanger upto his parent's house a little far off. Barnabus's gouty father, stout mother, and yellow haired sisters – Olga and Amalia greet him. The house is in bad condition.

Olga, the gentler sister of Barnabus welcomes K. to stay there for food. She assures him some beer which she is now going to bring from the inn Herrenhof. K. accompanies her there, and finds that Herrenhof is meant only for the Castle officials. He learns that the chief officer of the Castle, Mr. Klamm rests there.

Chapter 3 opens with Kafka's description of Herrenhof. K. meets a young lady Frieda and gets information about Klamm. An unobtrusive little girl with fair hair, sad eyes and hollow cheeks, with a striking look of conscious superiority. As soon as her eye meets K.'s it seems to him that her look decides something concerning himself, something which he has not known to exist, but which her look assures him does exist. He keeps on studying her from the side, even while she is speaking to Olga. Olga and Frieda are apparently not intimate. They exchange only a few cold words. K. wants to hear more, and so interposes with a question on his own account:

"Do you know Herr Klamm?" Olga laughes out loud.

"What are you laughing at?" asks K. irritably.

"I'm not laughing," she protests, but goes on laughing. "Would you like to see Herr Klamm?"

K. begs for a sight of him.

Frieda shows the peephole, and K. looks at Klamm resting, through it.

Klamm is a middle-sized, plump, and ponderous man. His face is still smooth, but his cheeks are already somewhat flabby with age. His black moustache has long points, his eyes are hidden behind glittering pincenez that sits awry. If he has been planted squarely before his desk K. will only have seen his profile, but since he is turned directly towards K. his whole face is visible. Frieda is Klamm's mistress.

Then K. has a few words with Frieda: "When can I talk to you?" "Can I spend the night here?" asks K.

"Yes," says Frieda. Frieda says, "Klamm will never talk to you!"

Both K. and Frieda grow into lovers gradually.

The landlady of the inn, apparently Frieda's mother, scolds K.: "'You are not from the Castle, you are not from the village, you aren't anything. Or rather, unfortunately, you are something, a stranger, a man who isn't wanted and is in everybody's way, a man who's always causing trouble, a man who takes up the maids' room, a man whose intentions are obscure, a man who has ruined our dear little Frieda and whom we must unfortunately accept as her husband."

The landlady says that Klamm never speaks to the laity in the village. Even he would not speak much to her when she was Klamm's barmaid cum mistress. But he allowed some freedom to Frieda. She asks K. to find out an inn elsewhere for better.

Chapter 5 is about K.'s interview with the Superintendent. He meets the man now ill at his home. The interview helps us to understand the castle village as a small feudal state, and its administration – all in disorder and confusion. Kafka writes, "So here is our Land Surveyor, he says, and tries to sit up. You've been taken on as Land Surveyor, as you say, but, unfortunately, we have no need of a Land Surveyor. There wouldn't be the least use for one here. The frontiers of our little state are marked out and all officially recorded. So what should we do with a Land Surveyor?" Though he has not given the matter a moment's thought before, K. is convinced now at the bottom of his heart that he has expected some such response as this.

Exactly for that reason he replies immediately: "This is a great surprise for me. It throws all my calculations out. I can only hope that there's some misunderstanding."

"No, unfortunately," says the Superintendent, "it's as I've said."

"But how is that possible?" cries K. "Surely I haven't made this endless journey just to be sent back again."

"That's another question," replies the Superintendent, "which isn't for me to decide, but how this misunderstanding became possible, I can certainly explain that. In such a large governmental office as the Count's, it may occasionally happen that one department ordains this, another that; neither knows of the other, and though the supreme control is absolutely efficient, it comes by its nature too late, and so every now and then a trifling miscalculation arises."

"This is news indeed!" cries K. "but I understand better still that a terrible abuse of my case, and probably of the law, is being carried on. As for me, I shall know how to protect myself against it."

"How will you do it?" asks the Superintendent.

"I'm not at liberty to reveal that," says K.

"You always talk of the one thing," says K., "that I shan't be taken on as Land Surveyor, but I'm Land Surveyor already, here is Klamm's letter."

"Klamm's letter," says the Superintendent. "That's valuable and worthy of respect on account of Klamm's signature which seems to be genuine, but all the same."

"Mizzi is quite of my opinion and now I am at liberty to express it. This letter is in no sense an official letter, but only a private letter."

"Right," said K., "then you'll just have to take my word that he is one. I had a sharp encounter with this Schwarzer on the very day of my arrival. Afterwards he made a telephone inquiry of an under-castellan called Fritz and received the information that I was engaged as Land Surveyor. How do you explain that, Superintendent?"

"Now and again you're taking far too simple a view of the case. I'll enumerate for your benefit a few of the things that keep me here: the sacrifice I made in leaving my home, the long and difficult journey, the well-grounded hopes I built on my engagement here, my complete lack of means, the impossibility after this of finding some other suitable job at home, and last but not least my fiancee, who lives here."

"Oh, Frieda!" says the Superintendent without showing any surprise. "I know. But Frieda would follow you anywhere. As for the rest of what you've said, some consideration will be necessary and I'll communicate with the Castle about it. If a decision should be come to, or if it should be necessary first to interrogate you again, I'll send for you. Is that agreeable to you?"

"No, absolutely," said K., "I don't want any act of favour from the Castle, but my rights."

Chapter 6 begins with K.'s problem of stay in the Castle. Before the Bridge Inn the landlord is waiting for him. Accordingly K. asks what he wants.

"Have you found new lodgings yet?" asks the landlord, looking at the ground.

"You were told to ask by your wife?" replies K., "you're very much under her influence?"

"No," says the landlord, "I didn't ask because of my wife. But she's very bothered and unhappy on your account."

K. becomes impatient, and begins: "You asked me, madam, whether I had found other lodgings yet."

"I asked you?" says the landlady.

Gradually the two adjust to each other. Gardana, the landlady, talks of her visit to Klamm, and his three presents to her. She was once his mistress as her daughter Freida later. She prides with it. K. then wonders as to how he should have Frieda's fidelity to him in his married life.

Chapter 7 begins with K.'s talk to a teacher in the inn. The teacher simply speaks of the Superintendent's complaint against K.'s rude behavior. Of course, the Superintendent is afraid that, if the decision in K.'s case takes too long, K. might do something rash on his own account.

But in his own sphere of jurisdiction the Superintendent wants to provide a temporary and truly generous settlement; it simply lies with K. to accept it. He offers him provisionally the post of school janitor. At first K. thinks very little of the offer, but the fact that an offer has been made seems to him not without significance. It seems to point to the fact that in the Superintendent's opinion he is in a position to look after himself, to carry out projects against which the Town Council itself is preparing certain counter measures. And how seriously they are taking the matter.

K. in consultation with Frieda accepts the offer of Janitar, at least, till the two migrate to some country like Spain or South France as Frieda wants. This reminds us Eustacia Vye's ambition to go with her husband Clym to Paris and live a fine life there in Thomas Hardy's novel *The Return of the Native.* Soon, the teacher advises K. to stay in the school with his wife, of course, doing a list of chores there, and eat at the Bridge Inn at the cost of Town Council. Frieda's want of some salary is however refused.

Chapter 8 is an elaborate description about K.'s visit to Herrenhof (where Frieda worked previously) for meeting Klamm. Yet Klamm does not appear there. Pepi has taken Frieda's place now.

K. meets Klamm's village secretary Herr Momus later (in chapter 9) Momus dispatches any clerical work of Klamm's which may become necessary in the village and as Klamm's deputy receives any petitions to Klamm which may be sent by the village. Quite unimpressed by the facts, K. looks at the landlady with vacant eyes, she adds in a half-embarrassed tone: "That's how it's arranged; all the gentlemen in the Castle have their village secretaries." Momus, who has been listening far more attentively than K., supplies the landlady with a supplementary fact: "Most of the village secretaries work only for one gentleman, but I work for two, for Klamm and for Vallabene."

Momus brings down a document on the table and stands up: "In the name of Klamm I command you to answer my questions."

"In the name of Klamm!" repeats K., "does he trouble himself about my affairs, then?"

"As to that," replies Momus, "I have no information and you certainly have still less; we can safely leave that to him. All the same I command you by virtue of my function granted by Klamm to stay here and to answer."

"Land Surveyor," breaks in the landlady, "I refuse to advise you any further, my advice till now, the most well-meaning that you could have got, has been cast back at me in the most unheard of manner; and I have come here to Herr Momus—I have nothing to hide—simply to give the office an adequate idea of your behaviour and your intentions and to protect myself for all time from having you quartered on me again; that's how we stand towards each other." The landlady suggests K. to respect Momus as he is Klamm's secretary. So his case may be examined.

Once the landlady compared Klamm to an eagle, and that seemed absurd to K. But it does not seem absurd now; he thinks of Klamm's remoteness, of his impregnable dwelling, of his silence, broken perhaps only by cries such as K. has never yet heard, of his downward-pressing gaze. Klamm seems to be a God-like figure. He is like Beckett's Godot.

Chapter 10 begins with K.'s search for meaning in his mission. Shortly Barnabas and his assistants meet him. Barnabus gives him a letter from Klamm. It reads: "To the Land Surveyor at the Bridge Inn. The surveying work which you have carried out thus far has been appreciated by me. The work of the assistants, too, deserves praise. You know how to keep them at their jobs. Do not slacken in your efforts! Carry your work on to a fortunate conclusion. Any interruption would displease me. For the rest be easy in your mind; the question of salary will presently be decided. I shall not forget you."

K. only looks up from the letter when the assistants, who read far more slowly than he, gives three loud cheers at the good news and waves their lanterns. "Be quiet," he says, and to Barnabas: "There's been a misunderstanding." Barnabas does not seem to comprehend.

K. asks Barnabus to carry to Klamm the following message: "The Land Surveyor begs the Director to grant him a personal interview; he accepts in advance any conditions which may be attached to the permission to do this. He is driven to make this request because until now every intermediary has completely failed; in proof of this he advances the fact that till now he has not carried out any surveying at all, and according to the information given him by the village Superintendent will never carry out such work; consequently it is humiliation."

Then K. and Frieda, and their two assistants rest at the school. Kafka describes how they are disturbed by snow as well as a cat in the night.

The K. family does not get up in time in the morning. Gisa, the teacher who comes, complaints to another superior teacher about this. The superior teacher objects to K.'s indecency and asks him to clear the place. K. however holds a fine legal discourse, and does not vacate. In a fit of mood, he dismisses his assistants.

"Frieda," says K.

She puts away the coffee-mill at once and goes over to K. at his desk. "You're angry with me?" asks she.

"No," replies K. "I don't think you can help yourself. You were happy in the Herrenhof. I should have let you stay there."

"Yes," says Frieda; gazing sadly in front of her, "you should have let me stay there. I'm not good enough for you to live with. If you were rid of me, perhaps you would be able to achieve all that you want. Out of regard for me you've submitted yourself to the tyranny of the teacher, taken on this wretched post, and are doing your utmost to get an interview with Klamm. All for me, but I don't give you much in return."

"No, no," says K., putting his arm round her comfortingly. "All these things are trifles that don't hurt me, and it's not only on your account that I want to get to Klamm."

Frieda says: "I won't be able to stand this life here. If you want to keep me with you, we'll have to go away somewhere or other, to the south of France, or to Spain."

"I can't go away," replies K. "I came here to stay. I'll stay here." And giving utterance to a self-contradiction which he made no effort to explain, he adds as if to himself: "What could have enticed me to this desolate country except the wish to stay here?" Then he goes on: "But you want to stay here too, after all it's your own country. Only you miss Klamm and that gives you desperate ideas."

"I miss Klamm?" says Frieda. "I've all I want of Klamm here, too much Klamm; it's to escape from him that I want to go away. It's not Klamm that I miss, it's you. I want to go away for your sake, because I can't get enough of you, here where everything distracts me. I would gladly lose my pretty looks, I would gladly be sick and ailing, if I could be left in peace with you."

K. however is keener about his job in the Castle village. He is waiting for messages from the Castle about his order, work and pay. It is a sheer existential crisis for him. Frieda loves him, and she is with him now just to marry him, and if possible to migrate to France or Spain. K. is worried about Barnabus, and wants to see him. But Frieda is envious of Barnabus's sisters Olga and Amalia.

However, K. meets the sistes stealthily and for a beief time. He speaks to Amalia. "You are always so sad, Amalia," said K., "is anything troubling you? Can't you say what it is? I have never seen a country girl at all like you. It never struck me before. Do you really belong to this village? Were you b[illegible] here?"

Amalia nods, as if K. had only put the las[illegible] questions, and then says: "So you'll wait for Ol[illegible]

"I don't know why you keep on asking m[illegible] can't stay any longer because my fiance[illegible] home." Amalia props herself on one e[illegible] of the engagement. K. gives Fried[illegible] know it. She asks if Olga knows of t[illegible] she does, for she has seen him with Frieda, and news like that is quick to fly around in a village. Amalia assures him, however, that Olga knows nothing about it, and that it will make her very unhappy, for she seems to be in love with K.

She appeals for confirmation to Olga, who has just come in with an armful of wood, fresh and glowing from the frosty air, strong and vivid, as if transformed by the change from her usual aimless standing about inside. She throws down the wood, greets K. frankly, and asks at once about Frieda. K. exchangs a look with Amalia, who seems, however, not at all disconcerted. A little relieved, K. speaks of Frieda more freely than he will otherwise have done, describes the difficult circumstances in which she is managing to keep house in a kind of way in the school, and in the haste of his narrative—for he wants to go home at once—so far forgets himself when bidding them goodbye as to invite the sisters to come and pay him a visit.

The sisters speak of Klamm as an enigmatic figure. "But we do often speak about Klamm, whom I've never seen; you know Frieda doesn't like me and has never let me look at him, still his appearance is well-known in the village, some people have seen him, everybody has heard of him, and out of glimpses and rumours and through various distorting factors an image of Klamm has been constructed which is certainly true in fundamentals. In detail it fluctuates, and yet perhaps not so much as Klamm's real appearance. For he's reported as having one appearance when he comes into the village and another on leaving it; after having his beer he looks different from what he does before it, when he's awake he's different from when he's asleep, when he's alone he's different from when he's talking to people, and—what is incomprehensible after all that—he's almost another person up in the Castle."

"And a man like Klamm who is so much sought after and so rarely seen is apt to take different shapes in people's imagination. For instance, Klamm has a village secretary called Momus. He keeps well in the background. People in the village swear that Momus is Klamm. That's how people work their own confusion."

Coley Taylor finds much absurd of the modern kind in the novel. He says this with reference to Klamm, "*The Castle*, beyond its environmental significance, is a bureaucracy, an institution; the difficulties that K. encounters are those any ordinary person experiences in trying to influence an institution. Klamm the inaccessible might very well be any captain of industry who has surrounded himself with secretaries and ceremonies to keep besiegers away; the Castle staff which works at cross purposes in its various departments might be any big business so overgrown that its various officials are ignorant of the work of others, or of the doings of their underlings."

In fact, Barnabus speaks of all officials being like Klamm. Olga adds the story of Sortini (not Sordini as K. mistakes it) who once insulted Amalia, and hence the whole of Barnabus family is treated as if outcastes in the Castle village. Clearly, Kafka had the Sortini incident in mind from quite early on, since Frieda's animosity towards Amalia is shown at their very first meeting, and that animosity expresses the difference between a woman who has gladly accepted love from a Castle official, and one who has rejected it.

At the point the novel begins to grow a bit boring with sub-chapters. The first of them is "Amalia's Punishment." Amalia is to blame for everything. Olga says, "That's why, on reflection, I can't take Sortini's passion for her very seriously, perhaps he sent the letter simply to punish her, but not to summon her." "I won't argue about Sortini," says Olga, "for the Castle gentlemen everything is possible, let a girl be as pretty or as ugly as you like. But in all the rest you're utterly mistaken so far as Amalia is concerned. I have no particular motive for winning you over to Amalia's side, and if I try to do it it's only for your own sake. Amalia in some way or other was the cause of our misfortunes, that's true, but not even my father, who was the hardest hit, and who was never very sparing of his tongue, particularly at home, not even my father has ever said a word of reproach to Amalia even in our very worst times."

The next sub-chapter is "Petitions." The father begins the petition; he starts making senseless petitions to the village superintendent, to the secretaries, the advocates, the clerks. Usually he isn't received at all, but if by guile or chance he manages to get a hearing, how the family exults when the news come, and rub their hands. He is always thrown out immediately and never admitted again.

"Olga's Plans" is also a sub-chapter. Olga is happy and even proud to speak of her brother Barnabus's success in securing a servantship at the Castle. Olga counts on K. She thinks it is because of K. Barnabus is getting some work as a Castle messenger.

Meanwhile, Jeremiah calls on K. and K. rushes from Olga's home stealthily. The old servant behaves independently. He tells K. that Arthur as well as he are harassed by K. and Arthur has put it as a complaint in the Castle. He mentions the doing as per Klamm's deputy Galater's spying measures. There comes Barnabus with the news that he cannot lay K.'s request before Klamm as there is much unease. Barnabus speaks of his visit to Erlanger, Klamm's one private secretary who says to Barnabus: "You know the Land Surveyor, don't you?" And then he says: "That's very lucky. I'm just going to Herrenhof. The Land Surveyor is to report to me there. I'll be in room number 15. But he must come at once. I've only a few things to settle there and I leave again for the Castle at 5 o'clock in the morning. Tell him that it's very important that I should speak to him."

Chapter 17 is about the political activities at Herrenof, the privileged hotel in the Castle village. Before the dark a little group of men are standing, two or three have lanterns with them, so that a face here and there can be distinguished. K. recognizes only one acquaintance, Gerstacker, the carrier.

Gerstacker greets him with the inquiry: "You're still in the village?" "Yes," replies K.

Momus interviews K. As K. is passing Momus the latter exclaims, "Ah, the Land Surveyor?"

"The man who was so unwilling to be examined and now is in a hurry to be examined. It would have been simpler to let me do it that time. Well, really it's difficult to choose the right time for a hearing."

Since at these words K. makes to stop, Momus goes on: "Go in, go in! I need your answers then, I don't now."

Nevertheless K. replies, provoked by Momus's tone: "You only think of yourselves. I would never and will never answer merely because of someone's office, neither then nor now."

Momus replies: "Of whom, then, should we think? Who else is there here? Look for yourself?"

Then, as he is looking round aimlessly, K. notices Frieda far away "at a turn of the passage;" she behaves as if she does not recognize him. K. rushes to her.

"She speaks angrily, "What do you want from me? Go back to the others - oh, you know whom I mean, you've just come from them, I can see it."

He learns that she has joined taproom. K. says, "But once you left the taproom for my sake, and now that we're soon to be married are you going back to it again?"

"There will be no marriage," says Frieda.

"You don't know what fidelity is," she says, his nearness putting her a little on the defensive, "what your relations with the girl may be isn't the most important point; the fact that you go to that house at all and come back with the smell of their kitchen on your clothes is itself an unendurable humiliation for me. And then you rush out of the school without saying a word. And stay with them, too, the half of the night. Tonight I only thought of dropping in there for a minute to see whether Barnabas had come at last, for he had an important message which he should have brought long before."

Kafka writes of K.'s tragedy: "Then someone called from the side passage, it was Jeremiah, he was standing there on the lowest step, he was in his shirt, but had thrown a wrap of Frieda's round him. This in fact was the effect that he had on Frieda. She disengaged herself from K., and was down beside Jeremiah in a second."

As Kafka narrates the story with suspension, Frieda loves her childhood friend Jeremiah now as she is bored, and even afraid of K.'s friendship with Barnabus sisters. Yet K. is faithful. Frieda misunderstands K. She is unhappy with K.'s mysterious attitudes.

K.'s separation from Frieda has an autobiographical colouring. In 1917 Kafka found out that he had TB and he could not live for long. So his lover Felice went off from him, leaving him in tears. Now he simply thought of his writing career. He stayed sometimes in sanatoria in 1922. He had also fallen deeply in love with a young Czech woman, the translator of some of his works, Milena Jesenska, with whom his relationship was easier than any he had known hitherto, perhaps just because she was both unhappily married and unwilling to leave her husband, so that Kafka and she saw little of each other and yet felt most tenderly. These were almost ideal circumstances, for a man placed as he was: here was a woman he could love, yet to whom he could not be married and who would thus not impede his writing. This new situation is reflected in *The Castle*.

Max Brod in "Aesthetic Effects," writes, "*The Castle* reflects, in a distorted form, Kafka's love affair with Milena, described with a curious scepticism and prejudice which perhaps offered Kafka his only way out of the crisis. Milena, who appears in caricature in the novel as 'Frieda,' makes determined efforts to save Kafka (K.), she unites herself to him, she sets up house with him in poverty and distress, yet gladly, deliberately, she wishes to be his for ever and so to lead him back to the freshness and immediacy of real life; but as soon as K. agrees, grasps the hand which she offers, her former associations, which dominate her, reassert themselves (the 'Castle,' her race, society, and above all the sinister Herr Klamm, in whom one may recognize a nightmare picture of Milena's legal husband, with whom she could never break completely), and their dreamed-of happiness comes to a sudden end. At the same time it is clear that in K. the will to radical salvation is even more uncompromising than in Frieda, who burns with too insubstantial a fire and too easily gives way to disillusion."

Frieda's strange jealousy and contempt of Olga are the counterpart to the attitude which, according to the letters, Milena adopted towards J. W. (Julie Wohryzek) to whom at that time Kafka was engaged. She categorically demanded that Kafka should break off all relations with J. W. and her family. Kafka himself regarded her demand as harsh and even unjust, but nevertheless he obeyed.

Here the text of the first German edition of *The Castle* ends. It has been translated by Willa and Edwin Muir. What follows is the continuation of the text together with the additional material (different versions, fragments, passages deleted by the author, etc.) as found among Kafka's papers after the publication of the first edition and included by the editor, Max Brod, in the definitive German edition. The translation is by Eithne Wilkins and Ernst Kaiser.

As a modern novelist, Kafka writes of rupture. As Jacques Derrida, the deconstructionist and Roland Barthes, the cultural critic speak of a gap between the tradition and the modernity.

After the great rapture, K. drinks heavily and wishes to sleep in a good bed "for ages." He is tired of life. Still he decides to meet Erlanger, but meets Klamm's another officer Brugel, who wonders at K. because he is not doing his work of land-surveying.

"I am prepared," Burgel continues, "to follow up this matter further. With us here things are quite certainly not in such a way that an expert employee should be left unused. And it must after all be painful to you too. Doesn't it cause you distress?"

"It causes me distress," K. says slowly and smiles to himself.

K. is now summoned by Earlanger. Earlanger tells K. that Frieda must go back to Klamm to serve him. He adds, "You are living with her, as I am told, therefore arrange immediately for her return. That is all I have to say to you." He gives K. a nod of dismissal, puts on the fur cap handed to him by the servant, and goes down the passage, rapidly.

This hurts K. who almost collapses at Herrenof. The landlady asks him to go. Pepi brings him some tea. Frieda arrives there to resume her former duty as barmaid and she does not care for K.

Kafka writes, "Frieda's luck brought the Land Surveyor into the taproom to her, perhaps on the very evening when the plan had come into her mind for the first time. The Land Surveyor! Yes, what was K. thinking of? What special things had he in mind? Was he going to achieve something special? A good appointment, a distinction? Was he after something of that sort? Well, then he ought to have set about things differently from the very beginning. After all, he was a nonentity, it was heart-rending to see his situation."

K. continues to struggle to work in the town and fights to reach the castle. On his deathbed, K. will at last receive a call from the castle granting him the right to live in the town in peace.

S. Oilman observes, "*The Castle* was written towards the end of Kafka's life. Another view of the novel relates its vision with Kafka's declining health: 'Indeed, the very physical presence of the castle looming on the hill overlooking the inn and the village suggests the isolation of the sanatorium.' The suggestion is that the scenario reflects the situation of Kafka's hospitalization."

But it is not Klamm that K. wants to meet, or rather Klamm is only a stage on the journey. Somewhere beyond, though only briefly mentioned, is the owner of the Castle, the oddly-named Count West-west. Is it the Count whom K. expects to meet? We are never actually told, and here one of the questionable elements begins to show itself: the reader is never told why K. wants to meet Klamm, whether he regards him as a final authority, or why he should think of destroying him. Part of K.' s purpose is clear—he wants confirmation of his appointment by the Castle as a surveyor.

'The Castle" is an allegory of man's search for divine grace: a troublesome, complex puzzle of man's soul, which is constantly teased, thwarted, and fascinated by a supreme authority which must be placated and obeyed. The Land Surveyor, of course, is a brother to John Bunyan's Pilgrim and a cousin to Peer Gynt. Mr. Kafka, however, while holding on to the necessary aloof atmosphere of allegory, has artfully and imaginatively made his Land Surveyor a modern figure.

Hans Joachim Schoeps writes, "The ultimate reason for K.'s failure is perhaps only this, that he cannot have faith and commits the error of trying to force Grace upon himself. For he lacked one thing during all his struggles, during all his life: the pious conviction, the hopeful confidence that what the castle would give him would be that which he considered good for him-that which eternity finds good. Therefore, because of his impatience, the Castle refuses to receive him during his life. When he finally breaks down, K. gains the painful insight. 'He who searches, finds not; he who does not search, is found.'

Kafka is attempting to say here, and elsewhere, that one cannot judge the demands of one's God in terms of rational being. It is in the acceptance of the irrational that one transcends rational ethics and enters into a hitherto inexplicable relationship with God.

Most responsible critics, from Marxists to Catholics, while disagreeing on other matters, continue to accept with no essential change the semiofficial interpretations of Max Brod and Thomas Mann in which the village represents "life, the soil, the community, healthy normal existence and the blessings of human and bourgeois society," and in which K. is seen as "driven on . . . by a need for the most primitive requisites of life, the need to be rooted in a home and a calling, and to become a member of a community." Or, as R. O. C. Winkler has put it more absolutely, "the hero's whole efforts are directed immediately toward an attempt to establish himself in a home and a job, and to become a member of the village community to come to terms, in fact, with society." In Herbert Tauber's view "The irony is softened by the fact that K. is surrounded by the villagers at the moment of his death. Even if his life was that of a foreigner, he now dies as a member of the community."

The Metamorphosis (1916)

The Metamorphosis: A Meditation on Human Feelings of Inadequacy, Guilt and Isolation is a great modern narrative. The present edition of Kafka's novel is a translation by Stanley Corngold of New York City. He is the author of a study of Kafka's *Metamorphosis* entitled *The Commentator's Despair*, and of a book of essays on German writers. He is currently professor of German and Comparative Literature at Princeton USA.

Kafka's short story "The Judgment" which marked a brackthrough into his mature style concerns a young businessman Georg Bendemann, with whom Kafka identified his own bourgeois personality. He decides to marry a lady with the initials F. B. Georg has a good friend in Russia in exile and somehow his marriage issue prolongs. Georg's father seems to be in destitution. Somehow this old man is changed from a feeble clown wearing soiled underwear into a haughty giant who reveals the news that it is he, not his son Georg, who really has a friend in Russia. Now the father rises up in bed to his full stature; and after accusing his son of an obscure fault, "radiant with insight," he proceeds to sentence him to death. Georg obeys.

In another story, "Wedding Preparations in the Country" Raban, the hero confesses : "As I lie in bed I assume the shape of a big beetle, a stag beetle or a cockchafer, I think. [. . .] The form of a large beetle, yes. Then I would pretend it was a matter of hibernating, and I would press my little legs to my bulging belly. And I would whisper a few words, instructions to my sad body, which stands close beside me, bent. Soon I shall have done – it bows, it goes swiftly, and it will manage everything efficiently while I rest."

Franz Kafka's small novel *The Metamorphosis* is a fine work in modernism. The novel has taken place as one of the most widely read and influential works of the twentieth century. *The Metamorphosis* was published first in German in 1915 in the journal *Die weissen Blatter*. It was translated into English by Ottomar Starke in 1915.

Unlike any other of Kafka's stories, *The Metamorphosis* is divided into three equal sections, each section ending with a climactic moment. *The Metamorphosis* begins thus: "When Gregor Samsa woke up one morning from unsettling dreams, he found himself changed in his bed into a monstrous vermin. He was lying on his back as hard as armor plate, and when he lifted his head a little, he saw his vaulted brown belly, sectioned by arch-shaped ribs, to whose dome the cover, about to slide off completely, could barely cling. His many legs, pitifully thin compared with the size of the rest of him, were waving helplessly before his eyes. 'What's happened to me?' he thought. It was no dream. His room, a regular human room, only a little on the small side, lay quiet between the four familiar walls."

Gregor thinks of sleeping a little so that he can forget this "non-sense"– dreamlike situation. He feels his salesmanship itself as a traveling salesman in fabric is a miserable job. He hates his boss. He says he does the work because he has to please his father. Probably he has to work to facilitate his father pay his debt to his boss. Maybe he has to work for the next five years. Actually now he has to go to his salesman's work. But the question is what to do now after the metamorphosis.

This is a piquant situation. Now the time is a quarter to seven. His mother asks, "Didn't you want to catch the train?" His father shouts, "Gregor, Gregor," and his sister pleads, "Is something the matter with you?" Gregor is sorry for them all.

Gregor thought he was in devil's trap. A parallel to the Faust legend suggests itself, with the important qualification that the 'devil's gift' to Gregor has been given him in his sleep.

The story opens with the collapse of this "riskiest moment" into the metamorphosis. There are no empirical events leading upto it, no attempts on Kafka's part to explain precisely why it has occurred, in what sense the change is deserved or otherwise intelligible.

Thus as Martin Greenberg points out *The Metamorphosis* has its climax in the opening sentence. The rest of the novella falls off from its starting point, its high point. Here, evidently, the traditional Aristotelian form of the narrative ceases to be relevant. *The Metamorphosis* generates its form out of its own fundamental subject matter: The traditional kind of narrative based on the drama of denouement—on the 'unknotting' of complications and the coming to a conclusion—could not serve Kafka because it is just exactly the absence of denouement and conclusion that is his subject matter. His story is about death, but death that is without denouement. For Clemens Heselhaus the metamorphosis calls to mind the *Metamorphoses* of Ovid.

But this "depiction" is anticlimactic: and in leaving the metamorphosis unexplained, it introduces another distinction between Kafka's and Ovid's fable.

Since the phrase "*ungeheueres Ungeziefer*" bears such a great weight of connotation in German, it is obviously impossible to translate satisfactorily into English. Among the previous translators of *The Metamorphosis*, Jolas renders it as "enormous bug"; Lloyd, as "monstrous kind of vermin"; the Muirs, as "gigantic insect." Heinz Politzer suggests "enormous vermin"; Walter Sokel, "a giant kind of vermin."

But at the same time Gregor did not forget to remind himself occasionally that thinking things over calmly—indeed, as calmly as possible—was much better than jumping to desperate decisions. "Seven o'clock already," he said to himself as the alarm clock struck again, "seven o'clock already and still such a fog."

Now Gregor thought of calling for help and laughed at his ridiculous change as absurd. Now he heard the office man's coming for his service. Kafka writes: "Something fell in there," said the manager in the room on the left. Gregor tried to imagine whether something like what had happened to him today could one day happen even to the manager; you really had to grant the possibility. But, as if in rude reply to this question, the manager took a few decisive steps in the next room and made his patent leather boots creak.

From the room on the right his sister whispered, to inform Gregor, "Gregor, the manager is here."

"I know," Gregor said to himself; but he did not dare raise his voice enough for his sister to hear.

"Gregor," his father now said from the room on the left, "the manager has come and wants to be informed why you didn't catch the early train. We don't know what we should say to him. Besides, he wants to speak to you personally. So please open the door. He will certainly be so kind as to excuse the disorder of the room."

"Good morning, Mr. Samsa," the manager called in a friendly voice.

"There's something the matter with him," his mother said to the manager while his father was still at the door, talking. "Believe me, sir, there's something the matter with him. Otherwise how would Gregor have missed a train? That boy has nothing on his mind but the business."

The Samsas are in trouble now. Because Gregor cannot get up. The manager is shouting outside and the boss may remove him from job. Not only that he may hound the parents for the old debts.

Martin Greenberg notes that sending for the doctor is the mother's suggestion, for she considers the metamorphosis to be an illness; and sending for the locksmith, the father's: he considered his son a nuisance, bent on causing him annoyance.

Now Gregor opens the lock and Kafka's description of the vermin's opening the lock painstakingly is beautiful.
Finally the vermin comes out of the room, the parents are shocked to see it. According to Hermann Pongs, the mother cries as if she too were beseeching God for His help against a satanic apparition. The mother suddenly gets into his father's embrace. The father has a cane in his hand, which frightens Gregor. The sister has gone for a doctor. The manager is outside. The father gives the vermin a hard shove which appears like salvation to it. The creature bleeds and runs into the room.

The second section begins with a description in the vermin's life, almost cut off from the world. Gregor's sister puts him a bowl of milk which the vermin does not prefer. The vermin still with a young man's sensibility notices the quiet atmosphere in the house which only frightens him. This is the same day's evening. None ever comes to see him. He could not sleep the night because of hunger and the worry how to rearrange his life.

The next day morning Gregor's sister visits him as of he is ill, or a stranger. She is surprised to see the whole milk bowl untouched by the vermin.

Kafka writes, "To find out his likes and dislikes, the sister brought him a wide assortment of things, all spread out on an old newspaper: old, half-rotten vegetables; bones left over from the evening meal, caked with congealed white sauce; some raisins and almonds; a piece of cheese, which two days before Gregor had declared inedible; a plain slice of bread, a slice of bread and butter, and one with butter and salt. In addition to all this she put down some water in the bowl apparently permanently earmarked for Gregor's use. And out of a sense of delicacy, since she knew that Gregor would not eat in front of her, she left hurriedly and even turned the key, just so that Gregor should know that he might make himself as comfortable as he wanted."

Gregor begins to eat the cheese and vegetables.

This then is the way Gregor is fed each day. The maid applies for the resignation of her job. The reasons are not clear. Maybe she is afraid to serve the house because of Gregor's metamorphosis.

In the course of the first day, Gregor hears his father worry about the family prospects. He has lost his business. His son then on struggles hard to bring comforts to the family. He begins his work as a stock clerk and becomes a salesman in fabrics.

In fact, Gregor solves the family's economic problem and his sister thanks him. Gregor likes his sister and her playing on violin though he does not like music. Now Gregor's father, though healthy, is old and sluggish. Mother suffers from asthma. And his sister, 17 years old who grows up luxuriantly cannot work. Gregor thinks of this with shame. The critic Edel underscores the fact that while it dawns on Gregor that he is cut off from all the others, while he loses his economic mainstay and is immured in his room by his father, his sister is in flight, even if in search of help—to be sure, from strangers.

According to Pongs, the mother cries as if she too were beseeching God for his help against a satanic apparition.

Gregor's metamorphosed life continues. His sister continues her soft service to him. Often the vermin would sit in the window (or even open it) and the sister would shut it. In that case he would sit in the couch. She, however does not like his shape. It repulses him forever, he thinks. So he pulls a cover taking four hours and sits under that cover. Kafka writes, "During the first two weeks, his parents could not bring themselves to come in to him, and often he heard them say how much they appreciated his sister's work, whereas until now they had frequently been annoyed with her because she had struck them as being a little useless. But now both of them, his father and his mother, often waited outside Gregor's room while his sister straightened it up, and as soon as she came out she had to tell them in great detail how the room looked, what Gregor had eaten, how he had behaved this time, and whether he had perhaps shown a little improvement."

One day Gregor's mother comes into his room. Grete is also there. Both cannot see him. The mother is even convinced that Gregor, the vermin cannot understand her. Now Gregor rules the bare walls. His mother is not used to the sight of Gregor. He is a little unhappy as his mother and sister Grete remove some furniture where he can crawl. Now he crawles on the walls of the next room where his mother is. The mother looked at the vermin and faints. "You, Gregor!" cries his sister with raised fist and piercing eyes. She collect a medicine bottle but breaks it down. The quaint smell of it disturbs Gregor.

Soon the father comes home. "What's happened?" are his first words; Grete's appearance must have told him everything.

Grete answers in a muffled voice, her face was obviously pressed against her father's chest; "Mother fainted, but she's better now.

"I knew it," his father said. "I kept telling you, but you women don't want to listen."

It is clear to Gregor that his father has put the worst interpretation on Grete's all-too-brief announcement and assumed that Gregor is guilty of some outrage. Now Gregor is frightened of his father. At one point, the father pelts Gregor with apple-pieces. Kafka writes, "One apple, thrown weakly, grazed Gregor's back and slid off harmlessly. But the very next one that came flying after it literally forced its way into Gregor's back; Gregor tried to drag himself away, as if the startling, unbelievable pain might disappear with a change of place; but he felt nailed to the spot and stretched out his body in a complete confusion of all his senses." This scene is poignant.

Section 3 opens with poignant details about the Samsas' treatment of Gregor. Kafka himself wounded in life speaks of Gregor's wound. He called his own tuberculosis the 'animal.' Kafka's own TB is hinted at in the story. Gregor's father did not like Gregor, as Hermann Kafka did not like his son Franz.

Economically the family is not comfortable: the sister takes a job in an office, the mother sews underwear for a clothing firm, the father becomes a bank messenger. Later an old maid works in the house and sweeps Gregor's room. She would say to the vermin: "Come over here for a minute, you old dung beetle." Kafka writes, "Gregor now hardly ate anything anymore. Only when he accidentally passed the food laid out for him would he take a bite into his mouth just for fun, hold it in for hours, and then mostly spit it out again. Look how these roomers are gorging themselves, and I'm dying!"

As we can discern the Samsa family inorder to face poverty; rents a room of the house where three people stay–often referred to as three lodgers or roomers. They are close to the Samsas. Once they like to listen to Grete's concert. So it is conducted. "Mr. Samsa!" the middle roomer calls to Gregor's father and without wasting another word points his index finger at Gregor, who is slowly moving forward. The violin stops, the middle roomer smiles first at his friends, shaking his head, and then looks at Gregor again. Rather than driving Gregor out, his father seems to consider it more urgent to start by soothing the roomers although they are not at all upset, and Gregor seems to be entertaining them more than the violin playing.

Somehow the roomers hate the creature. The father is alarmed at this. "My dear parents;" says his sister and by way of an introduction pounds her hand on the table, "things can't go on like this. Maybe you don't realize it, but I do. I won't pronounce the name of my brother in front of this monster, and so all I say is: we have to try to get rid of it. We've done everything humanly possible to take care of it and to put up with it; I don't think anyone can blame us in the least."

But Gregor has absolutely no intention of frightening anyone, let alone his sister. The following para reflects Gregor's misfortune and the growth of his tragedy: "And now?" Gregor asks himself, looking around in the darkness. He soon makes the discovery that he can no longer move at all. He still sees that outside the window everything is beginning to grow light. Then, without his consent, his head sinks down to the floor, and from his nostrils streams his last weak breath.

One day, the old maid, while sweeping, asks the vermin to come about. Alas! Gregor, the vermin is dead then: "Come and have a look, it's croaked; it's lying there, dead as a doornail!" The Samsas sit up in their marriage bed and have a struggle overcoming their shock at the cleaning woman before they can finally grasp her message. But then they hastily scramble out of bed, each on his side. Mr. Samsa throws the blanket around his shoulders, Mrs. Samsa comes out in nothing but her nightgown; dressed this way, they enter Gregor's room. In the meantime the door of the living room has also opened; where Grete has been sleeping since the roomers had moved in; she is fully dressed, as if she has not been asleep at all; and her pale face seems to confirm this. "Dead?" says Mrs. Samsa and looks inquiringly at the cleaning woman, although she can scrutinize everything for herself and can recognize the truth even without scrutiny. "I'll say," says the cleaning woman, and to prove it she pushes Gregor's corpse with her broom a good distance sideways. Mrs. Samsa makes a movement as if to hold the broom back but does not do it. "Well;" says Mr. Samsa, "now we can thank God!" He crosses himself, and the three women follow his example. Grete, who never takes her eyes off the corpse, says, "Just look how thin he was. Of course he didn't eat anything for such a long time. The food came out again just the way it went in."

The Samsa family is affected by Gregor's death. The father feels bad about the three roomers' objection to Gregor, the vermin's presence in the house. Hence, the father orders them to vacate his room. "They decided to spend this day resting and going for a walk; they not only deserved a break in their work, they absolutely needed one. And so they sat down at the table and wrote three letters of excuse, Mr. Samsa to the management of the bank, Mrs. Samsa to her employer, and Grete to the store owner."

Then all three of them leave the apartment together, something they have not done in months, and take the trolley into the open country on the outskirts of the city. The car, in which they are the only passengers, is completely filled with warm sunshine. Leaning back comfortably in their seats, they discuss their prospects for the time to come, and it seems on closer examination that these aren't bad at all, for all three positions—about which they have never really asked one another in any details—are exceedingly advantageous and especially promising for the future.

The Metamorphosis depicts the struggle between the son and father as it rises out of the oedipal conflict. And two phases of this struggle are placed hard by one another: the first, in which the son has the advantage, and the second, in which the father defeats the son. Between both phases stands the metamorphosis as the line of demarcation. For Helen Weinberg, who explores the underlying religious symbolism of the story, Gregor Samsa's transformation is quite literally a "negative transfiguration, the inversion of the Transfiguration of Christ, the Passion of an abortive Christ figure. . . .If this is the case," Weinberg continues, "then instead of *Metamorphosis. . . Die Verwandlung* would have to be translated, in the spirit of Kafka, faithfully and ironically, as *The Transfiguration...* indeed, even as *The Transsubstantiation...*"

In Helen Weinberg's theological reading of *The Metamorphosis,* Gregor is one who claims to be the Messiah. Gregor's narrow room, then, "appears on one level to represent quite concretely the womb of the Jewish imagination, which, it may be supposed, carries the idea of the Messiah in it but has not yet given birth to the Messiah itself and which has metamorphosed the image of Him who is generally considered to have come as the Messiah into the conception of a vermin, a monster." This reminds us the pig avatar of the Hindu god Vishnu.

At the time Kafka wrote *The Metamorphosis*, his own life situation resembled Gregor Samsa's just before his metamorphosis. This is revealed by several of his diary entries from the fall of 1912 and especially by a letter Kafka wrote to Max Brod on October 8, 1912, which caused Brod to intervene with Kafka's mother. Besides his work in the insurance office, which was hateful enough, Kafka also had to take on additional-duties in the factory belonging to his father and brother-in-law. Now all his free time for writing was gone, just at a time when, with "The Judgment," he had made a breakthrough into his mature literary style and needed all his time for writing. One may say his family drove him to despair and he was quite close to committing suicide.

There are, in this letter, a number of factors which went directly into *The Metamorphosis,* composed a few weeks later. Just as Kafka felt himself responsible for his family's factory adventure, Gregor, too, assumed the responsibility of paying off his parents' "debt" or "guilt" and is now being consumed by impotent resentment against this burden which enslaves him to his boss. As in Kafka's family, so too in the Samsa family there is no one except the unmarried son to rescue the family through toil and the sacrifice of his personal life. Suicide seems to Kafka a "rejecting" of all responsibility and hence a liberation, but at the same time a betrayal on all sides—a betrayal of the family and a betrayal of writing. In the same way, it is true, the metamorphosis is a rejection of all responsibility, but it is, at the same time, a betrayal of the family. As Kafka's suicide would rob him of the chance to test himself in both hostile camps—of literature and of life—so the metamorphosis cheats Gregor of the rewards which a conscious retreat into inwardness could bring him. The dominant element in both cases is bitterness and negative feeling toward the family, and guilt feelings toward it as well.

Kafka himself comments on the similarity between the name Samsa and his own, noting that this time he has come closer than he did in the case of Bendemann. The parents and the sister correspond closely to his view of his family, though only his sister Ottla seems to be included, and the sister Elli and Vally are left out. It remains, of course, a projection from his own circumstances.

Ralph Freedam writes, "Within this framework of realism and deliberate distortion Kafka's fiction evolves as a problem-solving activity. Man is confronted by a world of impossible dimensions and he cannot but despair of comprehending its overwhelming and mysterious forces. All he can do is to test—and to investigate the effects of his tests—his own capacity for understanding. Each fateful confrontation of the antagonists, self and world, brings with it hosts of mutually exclusive, indeed, paradoxical relations, riddles which seem to clarify but which eventually confound even further man's impossible task of penetrating the puzzling relations of his world. These 'riddles' are philosophical and theological, psychological and social; they extend to all spheres of human existence involved in man's search."

The Metamorphosis stands close to the line where the aesthetic reflection of meaningful human reality stops and the simple illustration of conceptual systems and dogmas begins; these have been, to be sure, intensively experienced and structured but they are hardly able to contain an essential and valid statement. Kafka's interest was always in the individual problem of the hero intensified to the extreme, while the conditioning social environment was illuminated by only a few – of course, frequently significant-reflexes [*sic*]. Kafka portrays human beings who have a fragile relation to the world around them; he brings this to light at an aesthetically pregnant juncture, then develops the conflict continuously until the catastrophe.

4

Franz Kafka's Short Stories

"Description of a Struggle," which was begun some time after 1902 and possibly as late as 1904, is Kafka's first significant work of prose fiction. It was never published in his lifetime - though some parts of it were recycled and published in 1909 in the periodical *Hyperion*. The story exhibits both the arresting originality of Kafka's fictional imagination and the remarkable individuality of his style. It was the first work that Max Brod remembered Kafka reading aloud to him: "I went about with Kafka for several years without knowing that he wrote."

"Description of a Struggle" refers directly to the specific topography of Prague in a way that was rarely matched in Kafka's subsequent fiction. The story feels like the projection of the fears and fantasies of the author. It opens with a closed domestic interior, an atmosphere of strange sexuality, an imagined 'friend,' who may be no more than an alter ego. In the section titled 'A Walk,' the imagination is seen as a countervailing force to the world of daily necessity, an escape for the dysfunctional individual ("Thus I toyed with my future life and tried stubbornly to forget"). In another passage, 'Conversations with a Supplicant,' the narrator declares, "of all these people who behave so irresolutely, so absurdly as a result of their confusion, I alone seem worthy of hearing the truth about myself." He later asks: "What is it that makes you all behave as though you were real? Are you trying to make me believe I am unreal. .. ?" In the 'Continued Conversation between the Fat Man and the Supplicant,' he notes: "contact with a human body is always repugnant to me." All these strangely juxtaposed elements clearly come from Kafka's own feelings, anxieties and obsessions at this time about where he fits into the surrounding world.

In 1909 Kafka finished the story "Wedding Preparations in the Country." Though fragmentary and incomplete, the piece is interesting, less abstract than "Description of a Struggle" and with much better observation of people and the real world. It is less a vehicle for private fantasies and anxieties, and prefigures *Metamorphosis*. The Prague cityscape of buildings and streets and the urban scene are precisely rendered: 'The horses stretched their thin forelegs, daring as chamois in the mountains.' The narrative plays with ideas of identity and of separating the real from the outwardly appearing self through word play on the German grammatical terms *'man'* ('one') and *'ich'* ('I'). The central character is travelling by train into the countryside to get married (leaving behind his other self, which has been transformed into a beetle) and some of his fellow-passengers are salesmen in the haberdashery trade (Hermann Kafka's, of course). Into a superficially naturalistic narrative, Kafka manages to inject a sense of unease, at one point declaring of the countryside, with abrupt mystery, "Nobody must dare to go there, but who could restrain himself?" Shortly afterwards the narrative breaks off because the rest of the manuscript is lost. Although this is frustrating, the work nevertheless shows Kafka's fictional skills being honed, and it points towards future developments in riddling, menaced narrative.

And the beginning of 1908 brought a fine compensation, Kafka's first publication. The bimonthly magazine *Hyperion*, edited by Franz Blei, published in its February issue eight of the very short prose pieces that would later form part of Kafka's first book, *Betrachtung* (*Meditation* or *Reflection*), published in 1913.

Brod's friendship was a source of great strength to Kafka. He joked with him about a plan to start their nightlife at five o'clock in the morning.

For the rest of his short life Kafka would struggle with the inescapable reality of his body, its failings, its dysfunction, its eventual collapse into terminal illness. He was hypersensitive to changes in his physical condition. He was a hypochondriac. He fretted about his diet, his constitution, his need for physical exercise.

In July 1910 Kafka woke one Sunday, after a night of interrupted sleep, to reflect on his 'miserable life.' His self-analysis now developed a new theme, which would culminate in the famous *Letter to the Father* of 1919.

This long drawn-out reproach is followed by a story, "Unhappiness," which centres on a bachelor who has insufficient involvement with the world to be able to withstand its shocks: "His nature is suicidal, therefore it has teeth only for his own flesh and flesh only for his own teeth. For without a centre, without a profession, a love, a family, an income; i.e. without holding one's own against the world in the big things. . . one cannot protect oneself from losses that momentarily destroy one."

In a startling image, Kafka writes of the bachelor that "his conduct can make one think of the corpse of a drowned man which, borne to the surface by some current, bumps against a tired swimmer, lays its hands upon him and would like to hold on. The corpse does not come alive, indeed is not even saved, but it can pull the man down."

Kafka wrote the story "The Judgment" (1912) in one night sitting on 22 September 1912. It was a breakthrough. Interesting as the *Betrachtung* pieces were, the bold narrative confidence and dramatic clarity of "The Judgement" signalled a leap forward in Kafka's fictional technique.

The story is simple to the point of non-existence. Georg and his father have shared a flat together since Georg's mother died two years previously. Apart from business and meetings over lunch neither man sees much of each other. Georg has just written a letter telling of his recent engagement to a friend in St. Petersburg and goes to tell his father about this. His father does not believe that Georg has a friend in Russia and the discussion escalates into the father berating the son until he finally bellows:

"So now you know what else there was in the world besides yourself, till now you've known only about yourself! An innocent child, yes, that you were, truly, but still more truly have you been a devilish human being!—And therefore take note: I sentence you now to death by drowning!"

At which point Georg takes to his heels and runs off to throw himself from tne local bridge.

This is an absurdist story that caricatures the relationship between father and son and the struggle for dominance and power—the father fights back from a position of submission by an eruption of power which ultimately destroys his son. Also, the father is outraged that his son is writing to his friend—another parallel with the real life of Kafka and his continual hang-up of balancing his writing with his other life. Alwin L. Baum, in his essay *Parable as Paradox in Kafka's Stories*, says: "As with Kafka, Georg's fiancee and his father come between him and the friend whose role is perhaps best associated with the estranged alter-ego of the writer. Like his father, Georg's friend is victim of his neglect, and has even "turned yellow enough to be thrown away."

By this, the father demonstrates that he has influence or control over every aspect of Georg's life.

In conclusion, the apparent power the son has over his father becomes illusory.

When Kafka made his 'trembling entrance' into his sisters' room to read the story to them while it was still fresh, Ottla said that the house in the story was 'like ours' to which he replied flippantly: "In that case, then, Father would have to be living in the toilet." But the autobiographical element in the story was obvious. In his first reflections on it Kafka also referred to "thoughts about Freud, of course." It is his first reference to the psychoanalyst, whose reputation was established firmly by this time, and the central importance of father-son conflict in Kafka's work generally might seem to sanction a classic Freudian approach to its analysis. Kafka, however, appears to make no further explicit references to Freud, though it is possible that the latter influenced some of the images in such stories as *A Country Doctor*.

There is something of Kafka in both Georg and in 'the friend from Russia' who fails as a business and is "resigning himself to becoming a permanent bache." The friend is in some degree an embodiment of the alternative Kafka, the path he might have taken (like that other man in East, the actor Lowy?), even if escape led to lack of success. Kafka later said that there was 'undoubtedly a great deal of uncle [Alfred Lowy] in "The Judgement." He also wrote later "The friend is the link between father and son, he is their strongest common bond. . . the father. . . uses the common bond of the friend to set himself up as Georg's antagonist. Georg is left with nothing."

His later lover Milena Jesenski translated this story into Czech.

In the middle of December, not long after the publication of a review of "The Judgement" (which Kafka always referred to as 'your story' when mentioning it to Felice) in the magazine *Bohemia*, in which Paul Wiegler (who had heard the then unpublished story delivered at a public reading in Prague on 4 December) called it the mark of "a great, surprisingly great talent, passionate and disciplined, which already has the strength to go its own way." In addition, the collection of stories —some of them eight to ten years old—*Betrachtung*, had just appeared at the end of November.

The book *Betrachung,* which Ernst Rowohlt published in 1912, was dedicated to Max Brod. It had 18 short pieces (some appeared in *Hyperion* and *Bohemia*). The pieces were exercises in the fictional imagination that exhibit Kafka's love of precise detail and infinite suggestibility.

"Longing to be a Red Indian," for example, comprises just one sentence, rapid as the gallop it describes, expressive of a desire to get the instinctual life on a proper harmonious basis, to be as 'instantly prepared' as the natural man who is adumbrated. In many of the other pieces the figure of the solitary, socially awkward, not at all *'bereit'* individual predominates. "Whoever leads a solitary life and yet now and then feels the need for some kind of contact. . ." begins one piece. Another starts: "It seems so dreadful to remain a bachelor..." and another: "I am standing on the platform of the tram and am entirely uncertain as to my place in this world, in this town, in my family." This is the world of Kafka at the age of 29, uncertain and anxious as an adolescent, envious of those who move in the world with spontaneous animal energy and vigorous confidence. The opening sketch of 'Children on a Country Road' injects an odd tone of unease into what appears at first sight a slight, impressionistic piece about children playing on a summer evening.

"In Unhappiness" which closes the volume and is the longest and most complex piece in it, we are once again in a claustrophobic domestic interior. In this story the solitary narrator encounters the small ghost of a child, who bursts into the room in an abrupt, dramatic gesture of a kind familiar in these stories, which echo the striking dramatic effects used in the Yiddish theatre or more widely in expressionist literature. There is also, as so often in Kafka's early fiction, a vaguely disturbing sexual dimension.

On 1 May Kafka told Felice that "a very short book of mine" was to be published in June in a new young writers' series from Wolff called "The Day of Judgement."

"The Stoker," the first chapter of *The Man Who Disappeared* and "The Judgment" appeared in this volume *The Sons* in 1913.

Now Kafka wrote the next three stories "In the Penal Colony" (1914), "Before the Law" (1914) and "The Giant Mole" (1914).

Kafka felt that "the beginning of every story is ridiculous at first as if it could not possibly survive," but "one shouldn't forget that the story, if it has any justification to exist, bears its complete organization within itself even before it has been fully formed."

When he offered "The Stoker" to Wolff in April 1913, Kafka suggested putting it in one volume with *Metamorphosis* and "The Judgement" under the title *The Sons.* The reason for this suggestion is obvious: all three stories concern the fate of young men, exiled, threatened or sent to their deaths by their fathers.

Kafka wrote "In the Penal Colony" when his marriage event was frustrated, and the war broke. The tale is a bit sadomasochistic. The story recounts the visit by an 'explorer' or 'voyager' to a tropical penal settlement where an officer is keen to demonstrate his instrument of punishment, called 'the harrow.' "Whatever commandment the prisoner has disobeyed is written upon his body by the harrow," the officer explains. Punishment is determined without fuss; there is no trial and the sentence is decided arbitrarily: "My guiding principle is this: guilt is never to be doubted." The condemned knows neither the sentence nor even the fact that it is to be carried out. "There would be no point in announcing it to him. You see, he gets to know it in the flesh." The long-standing debate about whether Kafka foresaw the fate of the Jews in Nazi Europe is revived by this story.

"It's a remarkable piece of apparatus," said the officer to the explorer and surveyed with a certain air of admiration the apparatus which was after all quite familiar to him."

Thus opens "In The Penal Colony," written in 1914 and published in 1919. As was Kafka's wont, there is little if no story. He invokes the atmosphere of the situation and captures, in detail, a telling moment in the lives of the characters.

Once again there is a death, lovingly described, but this time it revolves around the authoritarian officer and the demise of a defunct regime.

And here, almost against his will, he had to look at the face of the corpse. It was as it had been in life; no sign was visible of the promised redemption; what the others had found in the machine the officer had not found; the lips were firmly pressed together, the eyes were open, with the same expression as in life, the look was calm and convinced, through the forehead went the point of the great iron spike.

The officer had been the last in command of the Penal Colony being visited by the humanitarian explorer. The machine of execution being demonstrated to the explorer was the pride of the regime's authority—through execution comes enlightenment and acceptance of guilt. As if in demonstration of this ideology and recognition of the end of the line for everything the officer believes in, he submits himself to the punishment over which he presided.

Although there seems to be an initial reversal of Kafka's themes—the immovable higher authority in this case is crumbling—the work continues to explore authoritarian relationships.

K. Fickert observes, "Kafka continues in "In The Penal Colony" to employ the themes and figures firmly established in his earlier work the Old Commandant is basically a variation of the stern father; the dutiful son who sacrifices himself appears in the form of the officer. The traveller can be seen as a variant of another Kafka alter ego—the rebel, the opponent of the father, who observes the world of the older generation and rejects it.

Thus the characters in "In the Penal Colony" still conform to the Kafka blueprint. By presenting them in a different light, another perspective of the relationship of power and its use and abuse can be examined.

Within the story, thougn, there are different layers of comprehension. One of the more prominent metaphors is in the connection between the machine of execution and ritual Jewish slaughter or shehitah.

S. Gilman says, "The attack on shehitah as cruel and heartless compared to modern forms of ritual slaughter is echoed in Kafka's later story In The Penal Colony...However, the machine combines the modern forms of slaughter advocated by the opponents of shehitah, clearly condemning them, with the ritualism associated with shehitah."

The machine can also be taken in Christian terms. Rose Lawson sees the story as symbolic of the events told in the *Bible*. "In the Penal Colony" may be read as a thought-provoking fragmentary parallel to the crucifixion of Christ, in which the execution machine serves as an analogue of the cross.

The execution, according to the officer, brings about transfiguration in the condemned as they are tattooed with their sentence. Like the Christian story, the execution is about forgiveness and redemption. Thus the condemned are forced to accept their sin and are allowed into heaven.

Even though the old regime is seen to be on the verge of extinction, there is a warning enscribed on the Old Commandant's headstone: "There is a prophecy that after a certain number of years the Commandant will rise again and lead his adherents from this house to recover the colony."

Here is the potential danger of a resurgence of the old regime. The old powers could return, just as the power of the father returned in "The Judgement."

There are also sexual, sadistic and masochistic parallels in the story.

There is a strong link between pleasure and pain and the text explores this. The relish in the officer's description of the machine and the declaration that the process of execution will bring absolution presents the promise of pleasure. It also raises the question of masochism and sadism reflecting the fascination for torture. The explorer is both fascinated and repelled by the machine and its purpose.

"The Giant Mole" explores, among other things, the country and city theme, which was often on Kafka's mind.

In January 1915, Kafka wrote a story that he never finished called "The Blumfeld, an Elderly Bachelor" whose resemblance in the opening pages to his creator might be said to lie in their occupation of the usual claustrophobic domestic interior. Blumfeld is employed in a linen factory where he is an important employee. But he is often disturbed at home. The story then moves to an office setting which probably reflects Kafka's sense of the absurdities of his own workplace. Like Blumfeld, he could not conceive of leaving his office.

Taking advantage of his new writing-space in the little house in Alchemists Street, Kafka wrote throughout the winter of 1916-17, in a series of notebooks scholars have christened the 'blue octavo notebooks' (today they are in the Bodleian Library at Oxford). In this period he also wrote "The Coal-Scuttle-Rider," published in 1921, and stories such as: "The Knock at the Manor-Gate," parts of "The Great Wall of China," "The Warden of the Tomb," "The Bridge" and "The Hunter Gracchus," works that would not be published in his lifetime.

"The Great Wall of China," like the shorter piece "The Knock at the Manor-Gate," is concerned with the ineluctable nature of power and the powerlessness of the individual. Glancing perhaps at Prague's "Hunger Wall" started in the 1460s by Charles IV as employment for the city's destitutes, it is another story about organization; about the intricate procedures that govern how things get done; about work. "Almost every educated man of our time was a mason by profession and infallible in the matter of laying foundations," the narrator explains, reflecting the story's theme of the dominance of work in the modern world, our obsession with its all-absorbing futility. It describes the piecemeal construction of the wall, individual segments unconnected and built in the absence of any overall view of what was happening, as if it were a symbol of the fragmented modern consciousness.

"The Hunter Gracchus," which exists in several fragments, was written between December 1916 and April 1917, and is realized with the same precise accumulation of detail—another wonderfully original, strange invention, like a fairy tale or fable of death, its immanence. It is unusual in being set in a specific location, Riva on Lake Garda, which Kafka had twice visited. The army officer whom Kafka met in Riva in 1913, and who has been identified as Ludwig von Koch, was a retired major general in the Sixth Regiment Hussars of the Austrian Army. He shot himself on 3 October when Kafka was in Dr von Hartungen's sanatorium with him and his body was laid out in the mortuary chapel of St Anna at Riva. It is very likely that Kafka was influenced by this suicide when he wrote his story of Gracchus, who died 1,500 years ago yet exists in a halfway state between death and life. He arrives in a drifting barge at Riva, a soul who can find no permanent rest, like a suicide in traditional moralities.

Another story written at the end of 1916, "A Dream," appeared in a 1917 anthology called *Das judische Prag* and featured the first public appearance of 'Joseph K.' It is a wonderfully vivid dream narrative set in a cemetery, where Joseph K. meets an artist who is lettering a gravestone in gold. Slowly, Joseph K. becomes aware that the grave is his own and steps into the grave while "up above his name went racing with mighty flourishes across the stone." Another beautiful suicide.

Not long after, Kafka sent twelve of the new stories that had been set down in the blue octavo notebooks to Martin Buber for possible publication in his Zionist periodical *Der Jude*. He told Buber that they would eventually be published in a book to be called *Responsibility* (the title had been changed to *A Country Doctor* when the book appeared in 1919). Buber took two 'animal stories,' "Jackals and Arabs" and "A Report to an Academy," which were published in the autumn under Kafka's instructions that they should not be described as 'parables.' Kafka was in a much better mood and content with the flow of all this new work.

In his latest doomed attempt to uproot himself from Prague, Kafka announced that he was planning to go and live in Munich early in 1920. He seemed disposed to follow the example of his publisher, Kurt Wolff, who was relocating there from Leipzig. *A Country Doctor* was published by Wolff.

Kafka establishes an atmosphere of moral anxiety through the story of a doctor called out at night (he has no horse of his own but two emerge from nowhere to take him to his patient) to a young boy. In taking the horses and abandoning his maid to the violence of the groom who had brought them, the doctor is filled with guilt. The boy's open wound—described with Kafka's usual unflinching relish—is incurable, in part because of his extreme sensitivity, and part because he lives in a community which has lost its beliefs, an observation that suggests that it is to be seen as a spiritual wound, like Kafka's transformation of his bleeding lung into a metaphysical punishment. Kafka's view of medicine—the shortcomings of conventional doctors and the need for natural therapy where the spiritual is as important as the material in the process of healing—is entwined in this tale, which also draws on Kafka's reading of Hasidic tales, where some of its themes are echoed. Perhaps more than anything it is about the collapse of moral and cultural authority in the modern world.

Another of the stories, "Jackals and Arabs," finds a traveller in the desert being addressed by a group of jackals which has gathered in sight of the camp fire. It has a clearer intention of satirizing attitudes of the Jews towards their identity, and in particular those, like the Western Jews, who live at the margins of their societies and shirk the Zionist challenge to take practical steps towards improving their condition—in this case the jackals who rely on others to provide their food and want the traveller to cut the Arabs' throats and solve their problems for them. "A Report to an Academy" satirizes the assimilation strategy of many Western Jews, while Kafka satirizes himself in "Eleven Sons." He told Brod that the latter was meant to represent eleven of his stories, each of the sons being gifted in his way but unlikely to impress the father, who perceives in each "a kind of inability to develop to the full the potentialities of his nature which I alone can see." The father, like the conscience of a high-minded artist, is never satisfied. Many of the other shorter pieces, such as "A Message from the Emperor," reflect Kafka's search for meaning and certainty, his sense that it will never be found, that the message destined for him will not arrive in time.

Kafka and Julie wanted to go to Munich and live there. But Dora Diamant, a young Czech woman who wanted to translate Kafka's stories into Czech, held him back.

Probably around this time Kafka wrote the story "First Sorrow," which would be published in his last collection, "A Hunger Artist."

It is the tale of a trapeze artist who, as the only way of keeping his art at the pitch of its perfection, remains upon the trapeze permanently, day and night, with his needs supplied by attendants who haul up and down everything that is required. Like the lonely artist dedicated to his vocation, the trapeze artist was isolated from others who sometimes found his perfectionism a little trying his presence was a distraction during other acts, for one thing but he was tolerated because of his special gifts. The trapeze artist might have enjoyed this way of life for ever were it not for the need to travel from place to place (as Kafka the writer had from time to time to negotiate with the outside world and go to the office). The story exhibits Kafka's fondness for pursuing every last detail of his madcap invention—the trapeze artist hangs upside down from the luggage rack, for example, in the special compartment assigned to him while the circus is on tour. Then he suddenly announces that he is in need of a partner, a second trapeze, which the manager immediately grants. But the trapeze artist bursts into tears and cannot be consoled even though his wish had been granted: he cannot face performing on the single trapeze while the second one is on order. He then sobs himself to sleep while the troubled manager watches him, thinking, "he could see the first lines beginning to furrow the infant smoothness of the trapeze artist's brow."

The tone of the story implies that anything that is done through need should not be regarded as worthy. The side-show 'freak' is lauded because of his actions. The thrust of the story exposes this notion. Why should the public be interested in a man who is only doing what he does naturally? Taken further, this notion can be applied to anyone who stands outside of what society would regard as 'normal'—the artist or writer—for instance.

There are many absurd elements to the story. Putting on a public display of the act of starvation is a grotesque notion, yet there was, initially, an audience for it. The artist himself is not fasting out of choice and is not resisting temptation, even though there is an enticing parallel to Christ resisting temptation in the wilderness for 40 days. The artist is finally replaced by a more alluring side-show. Despite the signals, the story is "...show business. That is to say, the practising of welcome deception, for profit."

This story, like "The Judgement," has another, more personal drive. With "The Hunger Artist," it is as if Kafka is having a last, absurd rage against himself, his situation and his world. R. Hayman writes, "... obviously the story is developed out of self-criticism, whiie images of caging, chains and imprisonment were recurrent in his conversation. The 'I' is nothing ... but a cage from the past, its bars intertwined with incessant dreams of the future."

Kafka may also be taking a side-swipe at his friend Max Brod in the portrayal of the impresario who talks up the genius of the hunger artist.

It would be too obvious to link the metaphor of the food to Kafka's writing. It is possibly better—considering that he knew he was dying—to look at the food as a metaphor for the life.

Nicholas Murray thinks this is a typical Kafka short story: beautifully exact and told with the briskly straightforward pace of a realistic narrative, except that it is an utterly fantastic invention.

Kafka lived with Dora for some time in Berlin and wrote further stories. At around this time Kafka wrote the stories "A Little Woman" which was probably sparked by his landlady and conveys a sense of anxiety about always being judged even when the world generally is validating what one does.

Kafka had just completed "The Burrow," which he read to Dora. She was convinced that the story had a strong personal element and that it expressed a fear of returning to his parents' home. The narrator of this latest animal story is a creature who describes his carefully constructed subterranean labyrinth, observing: "I must have the opportunity of immediate flight, for despite all my vigilance may I not be attacked from the most unexpected quarter? I live in peace in the heart of my burrow, and meanwhile from somewhere or other the enemy is boring his way slowly towards me."

There are echoes of "The Burrow" in a story—"Investigations of a Dog"—written over twelve months earlier, in the autumn of 1922, when he was also ill and back in Prague from Plana. Another animal narrator finds himself "withdrawn, isolated, occupied solely with my little investigation. . . we are precisely the ones who live widely separated from one another, engaged in our peculiar avocations that are so often incomprehensible even to our nearest dog neighbor."

During that stay in Prague in March, Kafka had written a story, "Josephine the Songstress; or the Mouse People." The narrator, who speaks on behalf of 'us,' the mouse people, discusses the beautiful singing of Josephine. Like most of the other stories in Kafka's final collection, "A Hunger Artist," the concern is with performance. "Is it her song that enchants us, or is it not rather the solemn stillness which enfolds that small and feeble voice?" the narrator asks, querying the nature and purpose of art and its relationship both with a living community and with silence, just as Kafka would be pondering his own impending silence, his dying voice. The singer feels misunderstood by her audience no matter how much it displays enthusiasm for her art—"in her view she is singing to deaf ears" —and she "sings for preference in troubled times" with her "feeble vocal cords." The audience feels in some sense that "this fragile, vulnerable, somehow distinguished creature, in her opinion distinguished by her song, has been entrusted to us and that we must look after her." Josephine herself believes that "it is she who protects the people," that the artist has a positive function in society. In fact, "the thin piping of Josephine in the midst of grave decisions is almost like the pitiful existence of our people amid the tumult of the hostile world."

When Josephine claims she has sustained an injury her audience is unimpressed by this bid for sympathy—"if we were to start limping every time we got a scratch the whole people would never stop limping." She then starts to plead "exhaustion, dejection, feeling faint. So now we get a theatrical performance in addition to the concert." And then she finally disappears altogether: "Of her own accord she withdraws from song, of her own accord she destroys the power she has won over our hearts." The mouse people will continue on their way and she will be forgotten.

It is impossible not to read this story as anything other than Kafka's literary testament, his last word on the struggle to serve art and truth.

Kafka's Aphorisms and Parables

Kafka requires a metaphysical orientation, which posits a division between this life and a higher life, all the time he demonstrates the impossibility of surveying the line between them. For instance: "The joys of this life are not this life's joys," but our fear, he wrote, "of rising up into a higher life; the torments of this life are not this life's torments, but our tormenting of ourselves on account of this fear" (aphorism 96). In this sense, the goal of Kafka's writing is to probe the division between these two spheres, to worry and complicate it, and even to risk crossing over it.

Stanley Corngold observes, "Thereafter, Kafka does not think of writing as a type of philosophical reflections; instead, it constitutes 'a way,' a practical orientation. It is possible that writing might lead to the one goal that matters; 'to become a good man and answer to the Highest Court.' Yet it might also subserve a baser practice as, 'quite to the contrary,' it contents itself with a philosophical survey of mankind, striving "to know the entire human and animal community, to recognize their fundamental preferences, desires, and moral ideas, to reduce them to simple rules (or laws)."

A second aphorism concerns the knowledge of good and evil given with the Fall. Kafka's reflections on the Fall belong to an ancient tradition of biblical commentary but also to a German language reinterpretation of scripture that comes to the fore in the periods termed Classicism and Romanticism. This master narrative tells how the acquisition of the knowledge of good and evil spurs human perfection through the continuous exercise of reflection and judgment on things good and evil. It is sometimes called the 'triadic' view of ethical man and has been associated with Schiller, Holderlin, Kleist, and Novalis.

So what is the right response to the demand that comes with the Fall? It is, says Kafka, to do what one knows is required, act in the name of the good; for 'no one,' he continues, "can be satisfied with the mere knowledge of good and evil but must strive to act in accordance with it" (aphorism 86).

Around the middle of October, 1919 Kafka started to compose, in his blue octavo notebooks, a series of short pieces that have become known as the 'Zurau aphorisms' (some older editions of Kafka's writing print these separately as *Reflections on Sin, Suffering, Hope and the True Way*, but recent editions restore them to their context among longer, more reflective passages. They have the weaknesses and strengths of all aphorisms—occasional portentousness balanced by occasional terse insight —and are highly regarded by some readers of Kafka, especially those who see him as a religious thinker. A few representative examples (using a numbering devised by Kafka himself when he selected them from his original notebooks) would be: '38. A man was amazed at how easily he went along the road to eternity; the fact was he was rushing along it downhill' and '62: The fact that there is nothing but a spiritual world deprives us of hope and gives us certainty.

In his diary for the first two months of 1920 Kafka wrote a series of aphorisms known collectively as *He*, after the pronoun used in each, beginning: "Everything he does seems to him extraordinarily new." The aphorisms explore Kafka's senses of opportunity and constraint, the realization that progress is possible, but that he is at the same time a prisoner.

In his diary for the first two months of 1920—between 6 January and 29 February—Kafka wrote a series of aphorisms known collectively as *He*, after the pronoun used in each, beginning: "Everything he does seems to him extraordinarily new." The aphorisms explore Kafka's sense of opportunity and constraint, the realization that progress is possible, but that he is at the same time a prisoner.

If the 'he' of these aphorisms is not necessarily the historical Kafka, much of the detail, the angst, the worldview, is familiar: "He feels imprisoned on this earth, he feels confined. . . But if he is asked what he actually wants he cannot reply, for—this is one of the strongest arguments—he has no conception of freedom."

Brod recalled a conversation with Kafka of around this time in which the latter said: "We are nihilistic thoughts that came into God's head." Denying, however, the Gnostic view that the universe was a sin of God's, Kafka said that it was merely the product of one of God's mood.

"On Parables" begins with the famous complaint about the uselessness of parables. After all, all parables do is allude to "some fabulous yonder" but succeed only in saying: the incomprehensible is incomprehensible.

One man then said: "Why do you resist? If you followed the parables, then you would become parables yourselves, and thus free of your daily cares."

Another said: "I bet that is also a parable."

The first said: "You have won."

The second said: "But unfortunately only a parable."

The first said: "No, in reality: in parable you have lost."

The argument brings to the fore of recursive moment—the perpetual postponement, in principle, of what seems in every case to be the final claim. Indeed, there is nothing here to prevent the second speaker—or the reader who speaks in his name—from answering, "I bet that is also a parable." The parable, however, also contains an allusion to a victory of sorts, especially in the redemptive figure posed along the way: the man-become-parable, the body becomes the paradox of a 'truthful' writing.

5

Franz Kafka's Letters and Diaries

Franz Kafka as a great writer had the habit of maintaining diaries and writing letters. His lover Milena Jesenska once said, "the letters complete the oeuvre" of his writing. Kafka himself wrote to his follower Robert Klopstock in 1922 that "Letters can cheer me up, move me, or arouse my admiration, but they used to mean much more to me, too much for me to see in them now an essential form of life. I have not been deceived by letters but I deceived myself through them; for years I warmed myself in the warmth they would produce when the whole lot got thrown on the fire."

Kafka began cultivating letter writing from 1912 and the last piece he wrote on death bed is a letter to his father, regarding his ill-health. The earliest substantial texts by Kafka which have survived are also letters, to two school friends, Paul Kisch and Oscar Pollak. It is remarkable that while in fictin Kafka did not find his mature voice until "The Judgement" in 1912, his letters evince his characteristic wit right from the start. What is more, they explore themes which will preoccupy him in his maturity. The advice the 19 year-old gives to Kisch, for instance, on a story Kisch has sent him anticipates much of the artistic soul-searching in his diaries written in the years ahead: "A little tremor, a little mood, a little life (not little, but made little) wrapped up nicely in honourable German syntax nowhere hammered out of necessity—I don't have to write, but I'm writing-nowhere lived from the inside."

Six months earlier Kafka had written to Pollak that 'a letter is like a leading ram in a flock of sheep, soon twenty more letters will follow in its tracks' which Felice Bauer among others would understand all too well. Kafka's at times pained sense that real communication by letter was impossible—because the gap between what he meant and what he could say was too wide —is revealed in his first letter to Pollak to have its roots in the *Sprachkrise* ('crisis of language') of the turn of the century.

Kafka's letters are literary and they can be read along with his fiction.

Kafka began his relation with his main lover Felice with letters. His friend Max Brod, and lovers Felice and even Milena Jesenska all adjusted to his habit of letter correspondence. Julian Preece observes, "If the notion of a 'crisis of language' was a commonplace at this time, then Kafka's interest in the mechanics of the postal system, on which communication by letter depended, in collection and delivery times, in rates of postage and the relative speeds they denoted, in short the acts of sending and receiving written text, is all his own. It begins too in the first letter to Pollak. The occupations of his three most important correspondents should be borne in mind in this respect. Max Brod was an executive at the Prague Post Office. If Milena translated his texts from German into Czech, which was the reason she approached him in the first place, Felice declared on their first meeting that she liked nothing better than typing up manuscripts, an apparently subordinate feminine role. She worked moreover for a company which produced 'parlographs,' the forerunner to the dictaphone, transforming speech into text. There is a pattern to Kafka's choice of correspondents."

Sometimes, Kafka would miss a letter from others and visa versa. For example, once Felice's letter was missed and it was read by Kafka's mother. This was a love letter! So Kafka would at times use false names and *postes restantes.* Kafka wrote to Brod as Martin Salvat. His sudden change from *Du* to *Sie*—from the warmly intimate to the distantly formal—in the letter to Milena, which stands in such contrast to the gradual increase in intimacy culminating in the original change from *Sie* to *Du,* is not explained by encroaching frostiness or the gap. Kafka just knows that her husband might be reading. The letters to Felice teem with the hidden presences of others.

Most of these family letters, including the small collection addressed to his parents, which was discovered in Prague in 1986, are useful as biographical documents, sources of information on Kafka's life, which does help us understand his fiction, but which is, as he documented and dramatized himself to such a degree and to such great effect, of legitimate interest in itself.

Felice's responses and non-responses can be imagined; imagining them in fact makes up one of the joys of reading his letters to her, not to mention the letters to and from others about one or the other of them, which are included, quite rightly, in the volume *Letters to Felice*. What the brief and relatively few letters by the others about him show is how unusual and precious, or, in the case of his mother, perverse. As well as Greet Bloch and Kafka's mother, both Brod and his sister are involved; Felice appeals Brod for help and receives one of the two most revealing pen-portraits of his friend Franz; the other is by Milena, who was also in touch with Brod. The reader of the published edition of *Letters to Felice* is sometimes in the position of the cleverer reader of *The Trial*, knowing more than the epistolary protagonist.

Kafka complains to Hedwig Weiler, with whom he conducted his first and inconclusive love affair in letters. "What little use is an encounter in letters, it is like two people separated by a sea splashing from the bank." As he was writing to Weiler he was working on "Wedding Preparations in the Country," as well as the short pieces which would make up his first published collection *Contemplation*.

In his second letter to Felice she is asked to keep 'a little diary' which will tell him "the thousand things about whose existence and possibility I know nothing."

The appearance of daily literary production is deceptive. There were much longer fallow periods, when, for reasons of ill-health or mental indisposition, Kafka wrote nothing at all or very little. At other times, the autumn of 1912 is the most explosive, he wrote on two fronts at once, producing a letter or two per day to Felice, as well as "The Judgement," "The Metamorphosis" and most of *The Man Who Disappeared*. This left little time for his diary, whose function, what Hartmut Binder calls 'mastering' or 'coming to terms' with himself was taken over by letter writing.

Kafka also wrote many volumes of diaries. Which helped him for his fiction.

This intensive diary writing clearly laid the foundations for his first burst of mature fiction writing.

Yet the diary entries for January 1922, a mixture of sketches, reflections, images, and aphorisms, are ultimately far more revealing of his state of mind as he began *The Castle* than any number of whimsical musings, let alone a blow-by-blow account of how he wrote each chapter. What he gives us instead is an ideal of how the images began to explode his mind and where he felt they were trying to take him.

This makes diary writing, like letter writing, very much a literary form.

The two modes of writing are thus linked in numerous ways. Kafka's talent for observation is revealed in both; in reply to Felice wondering whether he took much notice of her at their first meeting, which pre-dated his first introductory letter by five to six weeks, he responds with several pages of description, which she would have found overwhelming.

The diaries too are full of vignettes from everybody life, but, as Binder stresses, all of them are noted for a reason, making it imperative to know the precise context, in his mental or intellectual preoccupation.

Most of Kafka's daily writings, however, are letters, which, in sheer volume, are approximately twice as long as his collected fictions – his novels, stories, fragments and aphorisms and three times as long as his diaries. He wrote to male friends, most notably Brod (1904-24), Pollak (1902-04), and Klopstock (1921-4), to family, especially his sister Ottla, to editors, and publishers, and to women, most notably Felice Bauer (1912-17) and Milena Jesenska (1920-3), but also Grete Bloch (1913-14) and Minze Eisner (1919-23) and before them all, in a bizarre dress rehearsal for the epistolary dramas to follow, to Hedwig Weiler (1907-9). These letters are both the most intimate texts Kafka wrote and, paradoxically, among the most public. We know for a fact – if they were sent – that he intended at least one person to read them which is not necessarily the case with his unpublished fiction. Even his diaries were never entirely private, as he read extracts from them to friends, and he handled them, together with "Letter to his Father" to Milena so that she could understand him better. Even the most intimate form of writing is always an act of potential communication.

Julian Preece comments, "Letter to his Father," never reached its addressee. It thus did not serve its intended purpose of explaining Kafka's point of view to his father in the row over his choice of fiancée number of two, Julie Wohryzek, in 1919. More than any other single piece of his autobiographical writing, however, this 'letter,' which Brod first published in a volume of fiction, has helped generate a powerful component of the Kafka myth; his subordination in classic Freudian manner to an overbearing father."

"Letter to his Father" is a hybrid literary document, a piece of rhetorically heightened autobiography. It reveals a poetic truth expressed with an equally poetic license and, as Walter Muller Seidel has recently argued, it portrays a small minded personality whose views are fuelled by resentment, prejudice, and insecurity, in what was to prove a lethal and all too common mixture in Europe at that time. The father of "Letter to his Father" is a satirical send-up; the boorish uncomprehending patriarch, forever comparing his son's easy life with the hardship he had endured in his own youth and the hard work which he never left behind. One of the keys to understanding the letter is to appreciate that Kafka junior was a second-generation migrant, whose views and self-understanding were invariably radically different from those of his parents. There are worlds which separate them.

The memorable phrasing and the bitter humour are not the letter's only literary features; the narrative perspective is carefully handled. Kafka explains his whole life, his upbringing, relationship with his sisters and mother, his schooling and choice of career, his writing, his religion, his place in society, exclusively through his relationship with his father, while deliberately ignoring all other factors. That this is a rhetorical ploy is clear not only at the end when he imagines his father's response and thus interrupts his own narrative perspective with another. It accounts for why he believes both of them to be both innocent and guilty, innocent from their own point of view, guilty from that of the other. This is ultimately a literary rather than a private truth.

It is, however, when we get to the gaping holes in the text that the two great letter collections, to Felice and to Milena, resemble the fictions most closely not only on account of their physical incompleteness. The greatest entrance in *Letters to Felice*, what makes them assume the quality of an epistolary novel rather than a collection of biographical materials, is that of Felice's friend Grete Bloch, whom Felice sought to employ as an intermediary and to whom Kafka transferred his attentions. This move makes him vulnerable to charges of Sartrean bad faith in his dealings with Felice. So Grete emerges a villain there.

While the letters which Kafka sent are at least complete in themselves, the *Collections* of letters, are, like the three novels, like the diaries, like the collections of unpublished short fiction, incomplete. Fragmentariness is an essential component of the Kafkaesque. Individual letters written by Kafka himself have got lost and, except in Brod's case, very little that others wrote to him has survived.

For Milena this has been done thoroughly as it probably can be: she has inspired three biographies, her collected newspaper columns have been translated into German and some into English. There is even an edition of her letters to others, pointedly entitled *Letters from Milena*. The revised edition of Kafka's letters to her includes her obituary of him, ıer letters to Brod about him, and a newspaper article by her which they discussed. In contrast, Felice was not a published writer and played no public role except that of Kafka's fiancée. A biography of her world, forty years after she died, probably be impossible though one of Dora Diamant, whose grave in East London has recently been identified, is in print under the title *Kafka's Last Love.* Kathi Diamant has brought it out.

The order in which the letters are presented inevitably affects our reading as entirely different narratives are constructed: *Letters to Felice* has all the trappings of a novel not least because some of the letters are not to her at all but all are somehow about her. The critical edition, on the other hand, arranges all Kafka's letters chronologically, which quite shifts the emphasis at the beginning of the correspondence with Felice. It also excludes, quite rightly given its purpose, those written by others. But it generates new insights.

Letters to Milena, more compact and more mature than *Letters to Felice,* are about the possibility of communication of two people understanding one another completely. Kafka is seductive, but not emotionally manipulative. Near the end of their correspondence, after a 15 month break, after an effect his failure to reach her, he writes of his hatred of letters because they can only increase the distance between two people, who can never express the truth to one another in writing; "How can anyone come to the idea that human beings can relate to one another through letters! One can think of a human being who is far away and one can touch a human being who is near, everything else goes beyond human strength."

Dora Diamant

Coming from these letters one might think that he could not write to a woman without flirting, that writing to women was a form of calculated flirting, but this is not so. The letters of Minze Eisner, the young student he met at Schelesen, reveal a quite different side. Kafka behaves towards Eisner as an older friend, never moves from *Sie* to *Du,* and advises her on her chosen career as a horticulturist, her training, and then marriage plans without a touch of condescension. He encourages her above all to break out of her provincial rural milieu, to be independent and get out into the world. Kafka repeats this role of mentor with the young Robert Klopstock and showers his sister Elli with advice on the right choice of school for her son.

Brod is the third of Kafka's great correspondents. There is no time when they were not writing to each other; Brod, in immediate recognition of his friend's unique talent, preserved every scrap of paper, letter or postcard from the time they met. The revised edition of these letters, which, uniquely for editions of Kafka's correspondence, includes some of Brod's own responses, underlines that Kafka wrote to Brod each year from 1904. In the first letter he gets himself into a tangle over apologizing for his absence at a ball; a fortnight before his death in June 1924 he thanks Brod for a book and last visit to Klosterneuburg. Many in between are classic pieces of prose which have made episodes in Kafka's literary events. The bulk of the letters to Brod, nearly two thirds, were written in the last third of the time covered by their correspondence between 1904 and 1924.

Kafka's last seven years would amount to nothing as much as another *Magic Mountain*, chronicling physical and medical details, the opinions of specialists, news on diet and body weight, reports on exercise, rest and fresh air. Finance is an increasing problem and Ottla is often charged with getting letters to his employers translated into decent Czech or with visiting the Director herself to discuss Kafka's sick leave or the possibility of retirement. In his last winter in Berlin, hyperinflation wreaked havoc with his financial arrangements and he was dependent on money sent by parents and sisters.

Like the diaries, letters give some indication of the extent to which Kafka noticed or was affected by current events, items which caught his eye in the newspapers, for instance, or great upheavals, like the First World War.

But the phenomenon associated with current events which absorbed him the most was undoubtedly anti-Semitism and his

Jewish identity. If this is a question of self-discovery before 1914, after 1918 it is more a matter of self-defense. Writing to Brod from Plana at the end of June 1922 he shows a rare grasp of a recent event. This was the assassination of the German Foreign Minister, Walter Rathenau, who was hated by the Nationalists on account of his talent, his business success, and the responsibility they imputed to him (quite falsely) for the unnecessary negotiated end of the war—unnecessary because Germany was undefeated in the field. Needless to say, Rathenau was of Jewish descent.

The Jewish theme takes up some of the most delicate but also amusing and sometimes trenchant passages in the *Letters to Milena*.

Kafka's diaries, sometimes the sketchpad for his fiction, sometimes an outlet for his feelings, a private vehicle for self-expression, are less voluminous and take second place to his letters or literary writing. Often Kafka uses the diary notebook for a fictional narrative, which possibly shows how the diary and the fictions went together, or it shows, more prosaically, that the diary and the fiction went together that the diary notebook was the first paper he had to hand when he wanted to write. However, Kafka's diary entries are inconsistent.

The letters' survival and their publication history mirror those of the more famous fiction too, Kafka's momentary destructive wish, which he had ample opportunity to carry out himself, applied to the letters with equal force. Readers had to wait until the 1980s for reliable editions of diaries and fictions and are still waiting for the five volume critical edition to be completed, which will supersede Brod's 1958 volume. Kafka's letters appeared with much difficulty in print only in the 1980s. Only *Letters to Felice* (1967) and the *Letters to Ottla and the Family* (1974) were delayed in a more normal way.

What does all this writing tell us about the novels and stories, which despite of interest in the life have to remain the focus of interest? Sometimes Kafka comments on individual stories, most notably on "The Judgement" and "The Metamorphosis." And such comments always add something to the understanding of a literary text. Looked at in this way, Kafka's work is anything but autobiographical. A further approach is to view Kafka's life as one of his greatest narratives, which is certainly what has happened in some more popular reception. There are key episodes and well-known formulations which have become part of Kafka-folklore, explored most recently in Robert Crumb and David Mairovitz's comic book for students *Kafka for Beginners*.

But what makes the letters unique is Kafka's talent for writing; what enhances their readability is their cumulative effect. The opening sequence of the *Letters to Felice* could hardly be bettered in an old fashioned epistolary novel.

6

Franz Kafka and Jewishness, Marxist Interpretations, Films, Societies and Websites

Franz Kafka and Jewishness

Franz Kafka is closer to the Book of Job than to what has been called 'modern literature.' His work is based on religious, and particularly Jewish consciousness; its imitation in other contexts becomes meaningless. Kafka saw his work as an act of faith, and he did not want to be discouraging to mankind.

Herald Bloom observes that Kafka is often studied with reference to Jewish religion and culture. This way of reading the texts tends to draw Kafka, the personality, back into the equation; "Think of the Jewish writer, and you must think of Kafka, who evaded his own audacity, and believed nothing and trusted only in the covenant of being a writer." This embodiment can be related to the notion of the Jews as a persecuted race. Indeed the link between Kafka and Jewishness, and interpretations of his work in terms of God, the Old Testament and the Jewish faith, are easy to make and easy to apply.

Of all the elements of Jewishness, it is the Kabbalah, a branch of Jewish mysticism, that Kafka's writing is associated with. Kababalist scholar Gershom Scholem says that: "Although unaware of it himself Kafka's writings are a secularized representation of the Kabbalistic conception of the world. This is why many of today's readers find something of the Absolute that breaks into pieces."

Kafka's commentary on this situation can be found in such stories as "In the Penal Colony." Richie Robertson states that: "What Kafka is doing in 'In the Penal Colony,' then, is imagining what an organic community based on religion would be like. It would give meaning to an individual's life at the cost of extreme suffering. Yet despite its harshness, it might still be preferable to a society in which religious values would have declined and nothing but an obsession with technology has taken their place." It is as if Kafka's work conveys the philosophy of the Kabbalah in the form of an extended aphorism.

Kafka learnt that the Christians disliked the Jews. In a letter to Brod at the beginning of May Kafka exclaimed, in response to the former's reports on the situation of the Jews in Munich, where he was staying: "What a terribly barren preoccupation anti-Semitism is, everything that goes with it, and Germany owes that to her Jew."

Even Kafka anticipated the Jewish holocaust. If Dora Diamant said that Kafka's writings were cruel, it is true. But the Christian world was crueler than his writings. Hitler's Nazism killed two of his sisters, besides many kith and kin, in the concentration camps.

Marxist Interpretations

For many readers, especially those who lived under extreme regimes, Kafka's work represented a 'real' world. Rather than presenting a psychological or esoteric world, his writing became representative of a world that actually existed.

The institutions of power are often portrayed by Kafka as harsh and heartless, as, for example, in *America*. According to Peter Heller, the Marxist critic, "One can interpret the fragmentary novel, which Brod entitled *America* as a critique of the frantic, ruthlessly competitive world of work, as a denunciation of the mechanized, enslaved and enslaving industrial society which grinds us all to dust in its inexorable economic and psychological *America* presents itself for Marxist criticism of Western capitalism. Kafka, in Marxist terms appears, to be an 'apologist for the petty bourgeoisie."

Film

Kafka raises more questions than he answers. His texts embody many issues that are of concern today. Kafka is not only fascinating to academics but he is also fascinating for individuals and other artists.

There are quite a few films and theatre productions out there with some connections of Kafka. Probably the best known recreation of a Kafka on celluloid is Orson Welles's interpretation of *The Trial* made in 1962. Although the story is tweaked in places, it is still worth viewing. It is a brooding film with distinctive touches by Welles. Even so, there is still the spirit of Kafka in the dark shadows. The director Steven Soderbergh made *Kafka* (1991), a fantasy loosely based on the life of Kafka and Peter Capaldi made a charming, Oscar-winning short film in 1995 called *Franz Kafka's It's A Wonderful Life.* With these examples, the film makers turn Kafka into his own fiction. Kafka becomes one of his own characters.

Adaptations of *The Trial, The Metamorphosis* and "In the Penal Colony" have been made by Steven Berkoff for the stage, and Alan Bennett has turned his charm upon Kafka in his two plays *Kafka's Dick* and *The Insurance Man.*

Societies and Websites

There are thousands of websites connected to Kafka. The web will provide a rich entrance to the phenomenon that Kafka has become. Some of the sites that are worth visiting are *Joseph K's Castle Page, Leni's Franz Kafka Page* and *Constructing Franz Kafka.* They offer interesting information and good links to other sites.

For a poststructuralist view of Kafka there is Jacques Derrida's reading of Kafka's short story "Before the Law." Derrida reads the story as parable about the failure of exerting one's rights through legal means. The translation of Derrida's work is published as *Dissemination* by Chicago University Press.

Most of the building significant to Kafka's life are still standing. There is a museum dedicated to Kafka in the house where he was born and there are Kafka walks that will guide you around his life in Prague. His little studio in Golden Lane by imposing St. Vitas cathedral in the castle is now a tiny bookshop. There is another bookshop that has an excellent range of Kafka's books in the Kinsky Palace on the Old Town square as well as the Kafka Society and the Milena Café.

An initial search on the Internet, however will provide over 30,000 websites with links to the author. According to the playwright Alan Bennett: "His work has been garrisoned by armies of critics with some 15,000 books about him at the last count." The critic Martin Seymour-Smith boldly states that Kafka ".... Has been both more widely influential and more widely interpreted than any other single modern writer. If he is not the supreme prose writer of the century, then he is among the two or three who are."

7

Franz Kafka and Others: Kierkegaard, Gogol, Freud, Husserl, Mann, Heidegger, Dickens, Melville, Hardy, Joyce, Hemingway and Bellow

Franz Kafka is greatly studied in modern times. He was a writer of the first order. This is based on an admiration of his mind and the genius of his art. Studies about his mind and art are furthered today. Kafka was an early student of the Danish theologian Soren Kierkegaard. Kierkegaard was a fine existentalialist.

Kafka's fiction *America*, *The Trial, The Castle, The Metamorhosis,* many short stories and letters and diaries, like James Joyce's *Dubliners,* speak of the modern man's demoralization, paralysis and degradation of the mind and body. His method is to adapt the general mode of symbolism to the use of parables.

Kafka starts with a general or universal situation. This being so, it does not matter where he begins his story, for the situation is always there, and always the same. Emerson says, "The way to the center is everywhere equally short," and Kafka might have echoed the thought in a different manner. As the situation is universal and stationary, it is also storyless; and this is the point at which Kafka's art begins. He is a great story teller because there is no story for him to tell; so that he has to make it up. In his three great stories the endings are indicated, but there is gap in each story, how or how small it is possible to say: and this does not matter.

Edwin Muir who has, with his wife, translated Kafka's fiction into English observes this with reference the Kafka: "The road then is there; we may imagine beside it a wayside inn from which an anonymous figure is just emerging. He looks ahead and sees, perhaps on a distant hill, a shape which he has often seen before in his journey, but always far away, and apparently inaccessible; that shape is justice, grace, truth, final reconciliation, father, God."

Kafka describes in *The Castle* the struggle to reach it, and in *The Trial* the flight from it. But the hero can neither reach it nor escape it, for it is enveloped, in a mystery different from the ordinary mystery of human life, and he does not know the law of that mystery. The frustration of the hero is an intrinsic part of Kafka's theme; and it is caused by what in theological language is known as the irreconcilability of the divine and the human law; a subtle yet immeasurable disparity.

In his letter to his father Kafka used the same method as he had employed in *The Trial* and *The Castle*; for what is so striking in them is the care he takes to state both sides of the problem; man's side, and God's. But the supreme originality of Kafka's work does not lie in his reading of the universal position, which he shared with Kierkegaard at some points, but in his story-telling by means of which he created a world. We can read *The Trial* and *The Trial* rejecting his theory of the irreconcilability of divine and human law, and yet find in them the most enchanting discoveries, the most startling riddles, and the most profound insight into human life.

The hero of the two great stories is anybody, and his story is the story of anybody. "Anybody" is obviously an allegorical figure, fit to be designated as K. or Josef K., or as Kafka names the heroes of *The Trial* and *The Castle.* Even the hero of *America* is anybody. All these novels, read like a trilogy, in fact in view of Kafka being the poster boy of modernism, plus his existentialist angst and Jewishness, studies are done of Kafka, in comparison with a host of other great writers and thinkers.

Soren Kierkegaard (1813-1855)

Soren Kierkegaard was a famous Danish philosopher who

influenced modern philosophy, religion and literature. He is regarded as the founder of existentialism. He studied theology at the University of Copenhagen. He is known for his criticism of Hegelianism on the ground that actual life cannot be contained within an abstract conceptual system. With this stand he wanted to reform Christianity. His works include *Either / Or* (1843), *Fear and Trembling* (1843) and *The Sickness unto Death* (1849). He attacked the organized church. His work strongly influenced the 20th century continental philosophers and theologians including Karl Barth, Karl Jasper, Martin Heidegger and Martin Buber.

Throughout Kafka's fiction the protagonist seems psychologically ill-equipped to deal with their situation yet muster all they can to do so. The philosopher Kierkegaard comments on this when he says he 'envisages man as caught in the dilemma of wanting to comprehend Divinity with the altogether inadequate tools of rationality.'

In a statement by Willy Haas: "Kafka goes back...... to Kierkegaard as well as to Blaise Pascal; one may call him the only legitimate heir of these two. In all three there is an excruciatingly harsh basic religious theme; man is always in the wrong before God." The work of Kierkegaard looked at the relation of thought to reality and helped pave the way toward Existentialism. Kafka's work reflects the Existentialist philosophy by the way it focuses upon the predicament of the individual, seeing him as powerless and unable to control his own destiny.

Nietzsche's endless questioning philosophy, as well, finds a resonance in Kafka's fiction. Both have examined the values of morality and a belief in God. Whereas Kafka's fictional world appears Godless, Nietzsche pronounced that 'God was dead.'

Nikolay Gogol (1809-1852)

Nikolay Gogol was born in an aristocratic family in Ukraine. He stayed in St. Petersburg with a literary ambition. He taught classes, wrote stories and plays. His play *The Inspector General* (1836) attacked the inefficient government machinery and his

Dead Souls (1842) criticized serfdom. In the end, he was melancholic and turned to religion. He died in gloom in 1852.

There are studies of Kafka in comparison with Nikolay Gogol.

But is Kafka so modern? There is a tendency to regard him as a freak among writers, a kind of novelist who could not possibly have happened before. We speak of the Kafka influence as though it were unique. And by "Kafka influence" we usually mean something extraordinary, grotesque, nightmarish, symbolic of modern frustration. Perhaps it alliterates so conveniently with Freud, and we prefer not to share this distinction of ours with those simple characters who knew it as *Weltschmerz* or even did not give it a name at all. Of course, the contemporary form of frustration is different but then, so is the contemporary world.

In Kafka's story *The Metamorphosis* Gregor Samsa wakes up in bed one morning to find himself changed into a monstrous cockroach. But Gregar Samsa is not essentially different from that unfortunate man Kovalev, in Gogol's story, who also wakes up (perhaps not unnaturally) in the same place (bed) and at the same time (early morning) to find that his nose has disappeared overnight, leaving a perfectly smooth patch in the middle of his face. The place and time are significant. For Gregor Samsa and Kovalev are awakening, not from a nightmare, but, reversing the normal process, into a nightmare.

Sigmund Freud (1856-1939)

Sigmund Freud was an Austrian neuron-psychologist and founder of psychoanalysis. He is one of the major intellectual figures of the twentieth century. He found out that mental disorders were caused by psychological factors rather than by organic factors.

Freud analyzed such concepts as free association, the unconscious, resistance and neurosis. He interpreted dream formation in *The Interpretation of Dreams*. He said dreams are the disguised expression of unconscious wishes. In his controversial work *Three Essays on the Theory of Sexuality* (1905) he spoke of Oedipus complex. He spoke of id, ego and superego, religion, myths and civilization. Despite controversies about his works, Freud remains the most influential figure in modern times.

Kafka and Freud were of one nation and were contemporary. Kafka learnt of Freud's great discoveries. Kafka's rebellion against patriarchy has much theory in Freud's Oedipus complex. The so called Freudian nightmarish experience was Kafka's too.

Martin Greenberg in his essay *Art and Dreams* draws a strong comparison between Kafka and Sigmund Freud: "Kafka's subjective world of apparent irrationality hiding a heart of meaning is Freudian through and through. His literal and mythopoetic quality is Freudian. His conception of the dream is in the larger sense the same as Freud's: both understood it as an expression of unconscious experience. Kafka was preternaturally self-absorbed and Freud or no Freud, he would have lived in his own subjectivity and dreams.'"

As we have seen, Gregor Samsa could be a symbol for the psyche of the Samsa family rather than a physically 'real' son. Equally, if one takes Kafka's protagonists as the only 'real' characters and the people they interact with as mere manifestations of the protagonists' unconscious, then we are presented with a new perspective of Kafka's work and the quests that are central to his writing. For instance, if *The Trial* were but a dream, then everything that happens to Joseph K. would be created from his subconscious.

Kafka had long ago acknowledged Freud as an influence on "The Judgement" and he had taken an interest in another Austrian psychoanalyst, Otto Gross (1877-1919), an early follower of Freud, whom Kafka had met at a party on 23 July 1917 at Max Brod's. At this party Gross had launched an idea for a new magazine to be called Journal for the Suppression of the Will to Power. His father had had him committed to a psychiatric clinic because of his drug addiction, and Gross was a possible catalyst for *Letter to the Father*: he was an advocate of revolution against patriarchy, which would be replaced by matriarchal power.

Edmund Husserl (1859-1938)

Edmund Husserl was an Austrian philosopher who established the philosophical method phenomenology. He studied sciences, maths and philosophy, and also Franz Brentano whom Kafka studied. Husserl taught at Freiburg from 1916 to 1929.

Husserl's basic themes are intentionality, reduction and life- world. Thought and action are essentially intentional in the sense of being directed toward the meaning of objects in the world and leading us back to the acts whereby such meaning is constituted. His abiding problem is to relate the pure ego to the life-world and to the inter-subjective life of individuals.

Thomas Mann (1875-1955)

Thomas Mann was a great German writer and a contemporary of Kafka. His first book *Buddenbrooks* (1901) brought him international renown. The Nazis condemned his books in 1933. Influenced by Nietzsche, Schopenhauer and Freud, Mann was interested in psychological and philosophical problems arising out of the individual's relations with the twentieth century society, which Mann regards as decadent. He is concerned with the role of aesthetics in the modern world. His *Tonio Kroger* (1903) is a novel about an artists' inner conflict. *The Magic Mountain* (1924) is a symbolic novel. It is his best. Mann is often compared with his fellow German writer Kafka as with Joyce and Proust.

Martin Heidegger (1889-1976)

Martin Heidegger was a famous German philosopher. He studied under Edmund Husserl, the founder of phenomenology. Heidegger taught at the University of Freiburg. In his famous book *Being and Time,* he defines man as a human reality. For him nature and society are instruments for man's satisfaction. Heidegger reinterpreted such terms as nature, fate, logos and art. He spoke of poetic and philosophical language. He analyzed Nietzsche's statement "God is Dead."

Charles Dickens (1812-70)

Franz Kafka read Dickens greatly. In fact, he said he based his novel *The Man Who Disappeared* (*America*) on Dickens's *David Copperfield* (1850). Dickens's father was an irresponsible clerk, and Dickens had to work as a child labourer. Then Dickens became a journalist and writer. He emerged a great social critic of Victorian England. His great novels are *Oliver Twist* (1839), *Dombay and Son* (1848), *David Copperfield* (1850), *Bleak House* (1853), *Hard Times* (1854), *A Tale of Two Cities* (1859) and *Great Expectations*. Dickens had an interest in social problems; capital punishment, the reform of prostitutes and the like. So prolific was his output and so frenzied his life, it seems miraculous he lived as long as he did.

Herman Melville (1819-1891)

Herman Melville was a great American writer, born to a bankrupt and insane father. He did a variety of jobs before piloting ships. He did a whaling voyage and by chance lived among the Typee cannibals. His fiction is about life on the sea. His great works include *Typee* (1846), *Omoo* (1847), *Redburne* (1949), *White Jacket* (1850) and others. Melville sympathized with pagan societies, developing a contempt for the white society. His *Moby-Dick* (1857) is about whaling expedition which is one of the greatest American novels, along with Hawthorne's *Scarlet Letter* and Twain's *Huck Finn*. His *Confidence Man* (1857) is a satire on American life. Melville's great poem *Clarel* (1876) is about religious crises, based on his trip to the Holy Land in 1857.

Thomas Hardy (1840-1928)

Thomas Hardy is one of the finest Victorian novelists, and pioneer modern poets. Hardy is second only to Charles Dickens in English fiction, past and present. He is a good short story writer as well. Who has not heard of Hardy's epic drama *The Dynasts*? Again like Shakespeare and Dickens, Hardy is a part of syllabus in schools, colleges and universities everywhere.

We find much similarity between Hardy and Kafka. Hardy is treated as a pessimist, sometimes. There is much truth in it. He spoke of the darker side of existence and people did not like it. They called him pessimist and gloomy. Hardy's novels like *Jude the Obscure* treat sex frankly. In fact, the novel was banned. It is said when Hardy stops Lawrence begins. Hardy's novel *The Well-Beloved* is a modernist novel. So is his poetry. Hardy was an experimentalist. Studies need to be initiated comparing Hardy and Kafka.

James Joyce (1882-1941)

James Joyce is a great Irish novelist. He was most unhappy with the rigid family life at home as well as the narrowness of Irish cultural life. He visited Paris in 1902 and was in exile much of his life. His book of stories *Dubliners* (1914) depicts this wandering. *A Portrait of the Artist as a Young Man* (1904), an autobiographical novel follows his own life from infancy until his first departure to Paris and it uses the stream of consciousness narrative technique. *Ulysses* (1922) deals with history and myth. His another work *Finnegans Wake* (1923) dissolves narrative into dream. Joyce's novels are modernistic, and they remain a living challenge to scholars, critics, readers and writers.

Ernest Hemingway (1898-1961)

Ernest Hemingway is a great American writer of the twentieth century. He is known for his direct and bold treatment of sportive themes of life. His great works include his short story collection *In Our Time* (1925), and many novels. *The Sun Also Rises* is about the disillusionment of the 'lost generation.' *For Whom the Bell Tolls* is about the loss of freedom anywhere as a diminution of it everywhere; and *The Old Man and the Sea* is a parable of inner strength and courage about a Cuban fisherman's struggle to bring home a great marlin he has caught.

It is instructive to compare some of Hemingway's best stories "The Killers," "The Undefeated" and 'Big Two-Hearted River"—with the stories of Franz Kafka, who occupies somewhat the same position in regard to influence today that Hemingway had between the wars. The two men have one thing in common; they are both masters of Naturalism. Kafka whom Austin Warren has called "a metaphysical poet in symbolist narrative," presents a surface which is strictly Naturalistic in detail, but he is dealing with a problem that is more complicated than the problem with which Hemingway deals: Man's relation to God, rather than Man's relation to Man.

There have been fiction writers in the twentieth country before him who concerned themselves with the same problem, notably, Hawthorne; but Hawthorne, important as he is, was never able to bring his material to the pitch of perfection which Kafka attained in his short life time.

Kafka's "The Hunter Gracchus," which though short, exhibits his fictional gifts in something like perfection. It is the story of the Christ who has been crucified but has never been able to ascend into Heaven. The artistic, as such, does not defend or criticize the myth of his age, he merely uses it. Kafka's subject matter is the scheme of redemption, as set forth in neo-Calvinist theology and the "philosophy of crisis," and his allegorical symbolism is as exact, if not as full, as Dante's. His scepticism shows itself occasionally.

Kafka achieves some of his finest effects by understatement. Salvatore in "The Hunter Gracchus," asks the hunter what port he will touch at next: the hunter says that he does not know. "....my ship has no rudder, and it is driven by a wind that blows in the undermost regions of death." Hemingway often uses the same device of understatement for the climax of his stories: "I can't stand to think about him waiting in the room and knowing he's going to get it. It's too awful," Nick Adams says in "The Killers" when he realizes that the two men in tight overcoats and black gloves are going to kill Ole Andreson. "Well," George the counterman says, "you better not think about it."

Saul Bellow (1915-2005)

Saul Bellow is the famous Jewish American novelist. He got Nobel Prize for literature in 1976. His great works include *The Adventures of Angie March* (1953) and *Herzog*. His *Herzog* as well as *Humboldt's Gift* (1975), describe the struggles of city dwellers to define their roles and responsibilities in modern world.

In *Herzog*, Moses Herzog, a 47-year-old scholar undergoes an emotional, intellectual and moral crisis. He writes letters to one and all, including God. He lives a disastrous life. He gets humiliated. He even thinks of joining a mental hospital. This theme demands a comparison with the Ks in Kafka's fiction.

One of the three fragments printed at the end of the definitive edition of *The Castle* starts: "Yesterday K. told us of the experience that he had with Burgel." An unidentified storyteller is introduced as the narrator in this fragment, and it is probable that Kafka intended to make another separate tale of it. As it stands, it comments on the elucidates the whole narrative venture that Kafka undertook when he started to write *The Castle.* The fragment ends: "And now I am going to tell you the story as well as I can word for word, and as much in detail as K. told it to me yesterday with all the signs of mortal despair. I hope he has meanwhile been consoled by a new summons. But the story itself is really too funny; just listen: what is actually so funny about it is, of course, his own painstakingly detailed account, and a good deal of that will get lost in my retelling it. If I could really bring it out, it would give you a full-length picture of K. himself, though of Burgel hardly a trace. If I could bring it out that is the precondition. For otherwise the story may equally well turn out to be very boring, it contains that element too. But let us risk it."

The nature of the Burgel story, which is not told by the unidentified speaker in this fragment, it to be comic, and its comedy lies in the very fact that K. tells it so "painstakingly" as if his life dependend on it. And K.'s life does depend on it.

Saul Bellow's Augie March declares when he speaks of the record he has made of his life story: "I have written out these memoirs of mine since, as a traveling man, traveling by myself, I have lots of time on my hands. For a couple of months last year I had to be in Rome.... Therefore I got into the habit of going every afternoon to the Café Valadier in the Borghese Gardens on the top of the Pincio, with the whole cumulus Rome underneath, where I sat at a table and declared that I was an

American, Chicago born, and all these other events and notions. Said not in order to be so highly significant but probably because human beings have the power to say and ought to employ it at the proper time. When finally you're done speaking you're dumb forever after, and when you're through stirring you go still, but this is no reason to decline to speak and stir or to be what you are."

Like *The Castle, The Adventures of Augie March* is the life history of a particular self. But *The Castle* is not a story of secular adventures but rather the depiction of an inner life through its manifestations in movements, gestures, choices, and acts in the world; *The Adventures of Augie March* is in this same pattern, as a close look at the novel itself will show, though on the surface. *The Adventures of Augie March* may be easily summarized as a "picaresque tale of a Jewish Huck Finn who bounces about the U.S. and Mexico sampling and quickly tiring of all manner of jobs, creeds and persons."

Still Kafka may be compared and contrasted fruitfully with many modernist and postmodernist writers of the world.

8

Conclusion

As we have seen so far, Franz Kafka is a great writer. He is studied as one of the best modernist writers. He is a neo-romanticist, expressionist and surrealist.

The present monograph on Franz Kafka is of introductory type for the Indian readers. The book has as many as seven chapters for a better appreciation of Kafka for modern readers.

The first chapter is about Kafka's life. Kafka was born in Prague, the capital of Czechoslovakia today. Then Prague was known as the 'secret capital of Europe.' It belonged to the Hapsburg Empire. It was ruled from Vienne. German culture reigned there. Kafka faced this paradox. He spoke both German and Czech, besides English and other tongues. The Germans disliked him because he was a Jew; the Czechs disliked him because he wrote in German. All people did not like him commonly because he was a self-loathing fellow. He was like his own Gregor Samsa, Joseph K. and sometimes K. of *The Castle* in search of salvation in the Gentile society. Kafka could not marry though he loved Felice and Dora Diamant and had expedited three engagements with ladies. Kafka suffered serious ill-health and as Milena says he dismayed himself. Nothing could cure him. Kafka wrote short stories, diary and fine letters. He was interested in Jewishness. He analyzed the material of the unconscious as a contemporary of Sigmund Freud. He made a criticism of the elite or capitalism. All this is discussed threadbare.

Chapter Two is a brief discussion of modernism.

Chapter Three is a critical analysis of Kafka's novels *America, The Trial, The Castle* and *The Metamorphosis* (which is a novella).

Kafka's first novel *America* which he called *The Man Who Disappeared*, is a fine fantasy in modern literature. Though it is least Kafkaesque, it speaks of his criticism of authority and power.

Kafka had wanted to write a novel along the lines of Dickens' *David Copperfield* but, in a way, it has more of a feel of *Pinochhio* or *Tom Jones* about it, in the sense of the 'innocent abroad.' *America* is generally regarded as Kafka's most cheerful novel. Michael Hofmann comments in his introduction to his translation of the novel that: "There is an opposing reading of *The Man Who Disappeared...* that, far from being a jolly picaresque or Chaplinade, its events actually describe a pitiless descent through American society, towards a probable catastrophe every bit as grim and ineluctable as those in *The Trial* or *The Castle.*"

Kafka finished *The Trial* in 1914 again incompletely and Max Brod gave it a finish in 1925. It is perhaps this novel which is most associated in the minds of the reading public with the notion of 'Kafkaesque,' for it begins with an arbitrary and meaningless arrest, and takes its protagonist through an intricate labyrinth of futile protocols. There is a clear connection between Kafka's state of mind when he began this novel and its content. The conclusion one derives from the long tussle with Felice—and it is still not yet over—is that Kafka felt himself to be a victim, like Joseph K, of some nameless, malignant authority or Law.

The Castle, written in 1922, again was an unfinished novel pieced together by Brod. The original publication of 1926 finishes in the midst of chapter 18; later editions after 1951 include the whole of chapters 18, 19 and 20. In one of its earliest notes, the title of *Temptation in the Village* was suggested by Kafka in his diary.

Like *The Trial,* the novel is effective in creating an overall atmosphere. Again, the story is episodic. K. has been summoned to the Castle to work as a surveyor, but on his arrival at the village at the foot of the Castle hill it is not clear what exactly he has to do or if he is actually needed by the 'Castle.' K. arrives at the Castle desperate to do his work, but he never does any work. He seems to be thwarted by the Castle and the village. Again, the notion of the individual's struggle between two worlds is evoked as K. is seduced by the Castle and village and his emotional connections with it.

The novel has spiritual overtones, as well as depicting a bad bureaucracy. The castle symbolizes an unbreakable authority of the feudal rule, or father or God. It represents the unobtainable. It can be seen as the idea of a nationalistic identity, existing purely as an abstract thought. The Castle stands as a journeys end. E. Heller thinks "The Castle is a terminus of soul and mind, a *non plus ultra of existence."*

Kafka's novella or the longest short story *The Metamorphosis* is one of the most popular modernist texts in our times. It reads like a cinema story where the hero Gregor Samsa who is tired of life turns into a beetle one morning. Then his family – his parents and sister—suffer on his account. Finally he is forced to die. The story depicts the struggle between son and father as it rises out of the oedipal conflict.

On the other hand, the tale does afford full internal evidence that Kafka meant Gregor's illness as mental and not physical.

Chapter Four is a study of Kafka's short fiction. As we know he has written more than fifty short stories like "The Judgement," "In the Penal Colony," "The Hunger Artist" and others. He published them occasionally singly or in small bunches like *Meditation*, *A Country Doctor* and *The Great China Wall and Other Stories*. Now they are available in collected editions. Like his novels his stories speak of the modern man's anguish and helplessness. His fiction deals with such themes as injustice, guilt, rebellion against authority and power, threat to man and futility. There is a strong line of absurdity in Kafka's work, exposing a deeper truth.

Then Kafka has written volumes of letters to his friend Max Brod and to his lovers particularly Felice Beauer and Milena Jesenska, and Dora Diamant. Most of these letters are brought out in book forms today. As well as he maintained diaries and they served him for writing fiction. This is discussed in Chapter Five.

Kafka was involved in many other things. As a Jew, he meditated on Jewism. He attended Jewish theatre seriously. Kafka was interested in criticism of patriarchy and power. His fiction, particularly *America*, speaks of his critique of capitalism. Kafka's works are adapted to stage and films today. Now there are Kafka societies and websites. This is discussed in Chapter Six.

Finally Kafka bears a comparison with many great thinkers past and present. He was influenced by Soren Kierkegaard, the most influential existentialist. Husserl and Heidegger (teacher-disciple once) had simiiar thoughts about reality, power and God. Kafka can be compared with eminent writers like Mann, Dickens, Hemingway, Melville and others fruitfully. This is discussed in the last chapter.

A Select Bibliography

I. Primary Sources

Novels:

Amerika (The Man Who Disappeared), trans. Edwin Muir, New Directions, New York, 1946.

The Trial, trans. Willa and Edwin Muir, revised, and with additional materials trans. E. M. Butler, Random House, New York, 1957.

The Castle, trans. Willa and Edwin Muir, with additional material trans. Eithne Wilkins and Ernst Kaiser, Alfred A. Knopf, New York, 1954.

Metamorphosis, Bantam Classics, London, 1915.

Short Stories:

A Country Doctor, Kurt Woolff, Leipzig, 1919.

The Hunger Artist, Die Schmide, berlin, 1924.

The Great Wall of China, Gustav Kiepenhauer, Berlin, 931.

Description of a Struggle, trans. Tania and James Stern, Schocken Books, New York, 1958.

Meditations, trans. S. Mortkowitz, Vitalis, 1938.

Letter to Father, trans. K. Reppin, Vitalis, 1999.

The Blue Octavio Notebooks, Exact Change, 1991.

The Penal Colony: Stories and Short Pieces, trans.Willa and Edwin Muir, Schocken Books, New York, 1948.

Dearest Father: Stories and Other Writings, trans. Ernst Kaiser and Eithne Wilkins, Schocken Books, New York, 1954.

The Complete Stories, Schocken Books, New York, 1971.

Letters, Diaries and Other Writings:

Diaries and Letters, Heinrich Mercy Sohn, Prague, 1937.

The Diaries of Franz Kafka, ed by Max Brod, Indianlog Publications, New Delhi, 2003.

Diaries II - The Diaries of Franz Kafka, 1910-1913, trans. Joseph Kresh, New York, Schocken Books, 1949.

Diaries II - The Diaries of Franz Kafka, 1914-1923, trans. Martin Greenberg with the cooperation of Hannah Arendt, Schocken Books, New York, 1949

II. Secondary Sources

Adler, J., *Illustrated Lives: Franz Kafka,* Penguin Books, 2001.

Anders, Gunther, *Franz Kafka,* translated by A. Steer and A. K. Thorlby, New York.

Auden, W. H., *The Kafka's Problem,* A. Flores, New York, 1946.

Berkoff, Steven, *The Trial and The Metamorphosis: Two Theatre Adaptations from Franz Kafka*, Derbyshire, Eng.: Amber Lane Press, 1981.

Bloom, Herald, ed. *Modern Critical Views: Kafka,* Chelsea House, 1986.

Brod, Max, *Franz Kafka–A Biography,* trans. G. Humphreys Roberts and Richard Winston, Schocken Books, New York, 1960.

Buber, Neumann, Margarethe, *Mistres to Kafka: The Life and Death of Milena*, London, 1966.

Carl, Frederick, *Franz Kafka, representative Man, Prague, Germans, Jews, and the Crisis of Modernism*, =

Carroughs, Michel, *Kafka versus Kafka*, trans. From the French by Emmet Parker, University, Ala., 1968.

Coots, Steve, *Kafka: A Beginner's Guide,* Abington: Hodder and Stoughton, 2002.

Diamant, Kathai, *Kafka's Last Love*, Basic Books, New York, 2003.

Eisner, Paul, *Franz Kafka and Prague,* New York, 1950

Fickert, Kurt J., *Kafka's Doubles*, 47-49. Las Vegas: Lang, 1979.

Fickert, Kurt J., *Franz Kafka, Life, Work and Criticism*, York Press, 1984.

Flores, Angel, *A Kafka Bibliography,* 1908-1976, Gordian Press, New York, 1976.

Flores, Angel, ed. *The Kafka Problem,* Octagon, New York, 1963.

Gilman, S., *Franz Kafka, The Jewish Patient*, Routledge, 1995.

Goodman, Paul, *Kafka's Prayer*, New York, 1947.

Gray, Ronald, *Franz Kafka*, CUP, Cambridge, 1973.

Gray, Ronald (ed). *Kafka: A Collection of Critical Essays*, Prentice-Hall, Inc, Englewood Cliffs, New Jersey, 1962.

Hayman, R., *K. A Biography of Kafka,* Phoenic Giant, 1988.

Hoffmann, Leonard, *Melville and Kafka,* Stanford, Calif., 1951.

Karl, F., *Franz Kafka, Representative Man,* Fromm International Pub Corp., 1993.

Kowan, Micheal, *Franz Kafka: Problems in Interpretation,* New Haven, Conn., 1962.

Lawson, R. H., *Franz Kafka*, Unger, 1987.

Neumeyer, Peter, *The Castle: Twentieth Century Interpretations*, New Jersey: Prentice-Hall, Inc, Englewood Cliffs, 1969.

Murray, Nicholas, *Kafka: A Biography*, Abacus, London, 2004.

Neider, Charles, *The Frozen Sea: A Study of Franz Kafka.* New York, 1948.

Politzer, Heinz, *Franz Kafka: Parable and Paradox,* Cornell University Press, Ithaca, New York, 1962. |

Politzer, Heinz, *Franz Kafka, Parable and Paradox,* Ithaca, N.Y., 1962.

Robertson, Ritenie, *Kafka: Judaism, Politics and Literature*, Clarendon, Oxford, 1982.

Salfellner, H., *Franz Kafka and Prague*, Vitalis, 1998.

Sokel, Walter, *Franz Kafka,* 19-22, Columbia University Press, . New York, 1956.

Spiers R., and B. Sandberg, *Franz Kafka*, Macmillan, 1997.

Spilka, Mark, *Dickens and Kafka: a Mutual Interpretation,* Bloomington, Ind., 1963.

Tauber Herbert, *Franz Kafka: An Interpretation of his Writings*, trans. G. Humphreys Roberts and Roger Senhouse, Yale University Press, New Haven, Conn, 1948.

III. Tertiary Sources

Bloom, Herald, *The Western Canon*, Papermac, 1994.

Bradbury, M., *The Modern British Novel 1878-2001*, Penguin Books, 2001.

Childs, Peter, *Modernism*, Routledge, London, 2009.

Collins, *Collins English Dictionary,* Collins, London, 1986.

Esslin, Martin, *The Theatre of the Absurd*, Penguin, 1991.

Faulkner, Peter, *Modernism*, Methuen, London, 1977.

Lodge, D., ed, *20th Century Literary Criticism,* Longman, 1972.

Seymour-Smith, M., *Guide to Modern World Literature*, Papermac, London, 1986.

Spector, S., *Prague Territories*, Univ. of California Press, 2000.

Index